D6 Family Ministry Journal

Published by Randall House Academic
www.randallhouse.com

D1430264

Heidi Hensley
Speaker, Author, and Children's Ministry Guru

Dr. Adam Clagg
Pastor, Author, Former Adjunct Faculty in Bible, Ministry, and Critical Thinking

Purpose Statement

The purpose of *D6 Family Ministry Journal* is to support the thinking and practices of parenting in Christian homes, in family ministry in the local church, and in parachurch settings that reflect God's intent for generational discipleship as presented in Deuteronomy 6 and other biblical texts. This purpose is achieved by the publication of articles and essays that do the following:

- Reflect on the scriptural foundations of God's use of paternal and maternal influences in the lives of children and grandchildren while also acknowledging various contemporary family situations
- Explore the integration and application of the relationship between the church and home
- Support the teaching of generational approaches to Christian education at colleges and seminaries for the equipping of ministry leaders and parents
- Champion methodologies that prepare children and young adults in the development of a Christian lifestyle and Christian leadership skills

The journal is primarily intended for two audiences: an academic community of professors and students in institutions of higher learning who are committed to the development of a new generation of Christian ministers and community leaders. Second, those professionals who are already serving in local church and parachurch settings. In order to facilitate discussion and learning among both groups, each publication will:

- Provide publishing opportunities primarily for:
  academic peer reviewed work
  practitioner reflection
- Offer a platform for research into family ministry
- Review new books connected to generational discipleship and classic texts and family ministry related fields

Manuscripts for publication should be directed to the attention of the managing editor at the following address: 114 Bush Road, Nashville, TN, 37217. Email inquiries should be sent to academic@d6family.com.

© 2018 by Randall House Academic
Printed in the United States of America
ISBN 9780892654710

Contents

Editorial

Articles

Practitioner Insights

Book Reviews

Editorial

In the ***D6 Family Ministry Journal***, the Randall House leadership, most notably Ron Hunter, Executive Editor, and Michelle Orr, General Editor, is striking resounding chords that resonate with the Christian academic community. The reader will notice, following the success of the first two editions, the third edition has garnered authors from New Orleans to North Carolina to Nova Scotia and from Michigan to California. These voices are expressing important themes that reflect both biblical thinking and exceptional academic research.

In this edition's first article, by Drs. Ken Coley and John Turner, the authors return to a very familiar refrain at the heart of all Randall House Publications: the application of Deuteronomy 6 in our 21st Century contexts. This article presents the remarkable connection between the truths established in the Pentateuch which are highlighted by current mind, brain, and education research. This is a must-read for pastoral leaders and parents alike.

Dr. Chris Hulshof next leads us into a discussion about the responsibilities of the good shepherd pastor. Building a strong foundation on John 10, Hulshof argues that the good shepherd pastor is, indeed, one who is a disability-effective pastor. Scripture shows us God's compassion for and desire to include those with disabilities throughout its pages, including numerous occasions where Jesus himself interacts with someone who is disabled, demonstrating four important relational qualities of the disability-effective pastor: intimacy, trust, accessibility, and sacrifice.

While Hulshof exhorts pastors to better understand and be prepared to minister to those with disabilities, Dr. Brian Haack zeros in on autism-specific research. Haack takes his survey tools to volunteers and children's ministry staff to understand why data shows such a low participation rate in local churches among those with autism, specifically children. Identifying the problem is only part of the battle, though, as Haack notes. He ends his study by providing some practical applications as he encourages churches to engage not only those affected by autism, but any demographic which may experience some social distance within the church.

While Haack has addressed the implicit attitude towards those with autism in our churches, Uranga-Hernandez tells the stories of four children with autism in four different churches to bring to light the struggles of not only the children, but their families. The statistics that she cites to show the specific hardships of autism-affected families (including depression and divorce, among others) also show a strong correlation between these same families and an interest in spirituality. So, she says, it is time for churches to prepare and provide the right resources and urges more research on the topic so that we can better love our neighbors as ourselves.

As Hulshof, Haack, and Hernandez implore us to prepare for and minister to families with special needs, Dr. David Kruse takes us a step back to examine just what are the needs of these families? Once the church becomes aware of this demographic, it cannot simply say, "Welcome." As God created these men and women in His image and is entrusting them to our care, so we should share in His love and dedication to engage them. And just as Kruse is understanding about the various potential disruptions and inconveniences in establishing a special needs ministry, he is equally as vehement about overcoming these challenges for the sake of these important families in our midst.

Moten and Clark each examine a different angle of what special needs may look like in your church, while Willhauck and Dean round out the harmony by offering their observations of how various familial relations can impact the spiritual life of the next generation. With more and more research enlightening us to various important factors in discipleship, verses are continually added to the song; but the chorus stays the same: "Hear, O Israel: The Lord our God, the Lord is One. Love the Lord your God with all your heart and with all your soul and with all your strength. These commandments that I give you today are to be on your hearts. Impress them on your children. Talk about them when you sit at home and when you walk along the road, when you lie down and when you get up."

Ken Coley
Managing Editor

Examining Deuteronomy 6 Through the Lens of 21st Century Educational Concepts

Dr. Kenneth S. Coley and Dr. John Turner

Abstract: The truths found in Deuteronomy 6 are both eternal and practical in their application to discipling the next generation—as true now as in the day they were spoken by Moses. The two authors of this research article, one a life-long educator and one a biblical scholar, revisit the biblical text and introduce current pedagogical insights and trends that resonate with the powerful concepts embedded in verses 4-9. Educational concepts presented in the article include connecting with the learner's schema; active learning techniques; practice that is spaced, varied, and interleaved; and cognitive and educational research findings that point to effective teaching strategies. Implications for parenting, discipling, and leading church ministries are presented.

Introduction

The co-authors of this article met in the summer of 2017 at Ukraine Baptist Theological Seminary in L'viv. One was packing to go home after a week of teaching current educational trends and issues to Ukrainian graduate students; the other was returning to L'viv for his fourth season of teaching Old Testament to college students. At first glance, the two seemed to have little in common other than being Americans visiting Eastern Europe for the purpose of teaching. They began sharing research interests over dinner that evening and discovered that the biblical scholar's passion for the Holy Land intersected with the educator's fascination with the apparent contemporary relevance of teaching techniques described in Deuteronomy. So, the seeds of this research article were planted.

Thesis

The phrase *teach these things to your children* spoken by Moses reverberates throughout the Old and New Testaments, is echoed in synagogues, monasteries, and cathedrals of the early church, and still resonates in the body of Christ today. Referred to as *discipleship, mentorship, apprenticeship*, and other terminology, the biblical mandate remains the same—instill in the next generations the love of God (heart, soul, and might). This article revisits the teaching process as described by Moses in Deuteronomy 6:3-9, and examines the specific instructions he presented to his people prior to their entering the Promised Land. The co-authors will apply different principles and tools in their shared examination. The biblical exegesis will be conducted by Turner, while Coley will use his educational training to view the passage through the lens of current educational trends and issues, including mind, brain, and education research. The question the co-authors are both asking is this—to what extent, if any, are the approaches to teaching younger generations biblical truth supported by current educational literature? Stated another way, would comparing a selected body of educational literature enrich our understanding of the Deuteronomy text and the specific instructions spoken by Moses? The researchers declare their bias upfront—we are not looking to current research in any field to validate Scripture. God's Word needs no validation.

Methodology

The content analysis of the biblical passage was carried out using standard hermeneutical techniques. The authors selected educational concepts for analysis and comparison that meet a number of standards. First, the concept must have a clear intersection with the text. A number of current themes in education were not included because their inclusion would have been on the basis of "we think this concept is implied," "this is based on an argument from silence," or "this concept is consistent with the discussion in this verse." For example, the concept of *formative assessment* is almost unmatched in frequency of studies, but the authors cannot claim that parents are to evaluate their children's level of understanding based explicitly on the text. Second, only those topics that are receiving wide acceptance in the 21ˢᵗ century were included. Third, the authors chose educational trends that are established as effective methodologies based on multiple research studies and expert endorsement. Space will not permit a discussion of the research designs that led researchers to conclusions regarding each concept. However, the authors include references that have ample details to support the findings introduced in this article.

Hear, O Israel! (verse 4)

Talk about a context for learning readiness! Imagine adult sons and daughters rushing to the death bed of their beloved father. They know he is about to impart his last words. How motivated are they to cling to every syllable? This image illustrates an urgent reality in the historical context of the book of Deuteronomy.

Moses knew he was about to die. He had known God intimately (Ex. 33:11; Deut. 34:10) and waivered not in the belief that I AM would faithfully bring His chosen nation into the land He had promised Abraham. Moses also knew himself. He agonized over the way he had publicly disobeyed God, disqualifying himself from crossing the Jordan (Num. 20:1-13; Deut. 3:23-28). Moses knew these children of Israel. He had watched their parents die in the wilderness because of their stiff necks, stubbornness, and unbelief. Now, he yearned for this generation and each one after them to learn from the past with reverence, set their hearts to remember the Lord's commands, and walk with faithfulness in the blessings of the Covenant. If they did this, Moses knew that Israel would glorify the one true God and bless every nation on earth (Gen. 12:1-3; Deut. 4:1-9).

Finally, Moses knew the last words God wanted him to speak. They were so critical and far-reaching—the difference between life and death—that he wrote them on a scroll and commanded the priests to carry the *devarim* (words) alongside the Ark that contained the Ten Commandments. He ordered the people to gather and read aloud the entire scroll every seven years at the Feast of Booths. They were never to forget (Deut. 31:1-13; 32:45-47). As Moses admonished Israel to *shema* (hear), he meant more than just *listen. Shema* also means *obey.* Moses longed for Israel to be doers, not just hearers, of his divinely inspired instructions. Moses' last words are entitled *Devarim* in the Hebrew Scriptures. *These are the Words* (Deut. 1:1) we know as the book of Deuteronomy.

Engagement

Ultimately, the church's greatest desire is for each person, young or old, to receive Christ in order for the Holy Spirit to indwell his heart. But until this supernatural change begins, how is it that we hope to inspire our children to obey? First, there must be *change*—in perspective, attitude, knowledge, and ultimately outward behavior. In every current discussion of effective teaching one sees the concept of engaging the learners in active participation in the teaching-learning process as the way to attain the most significant gains in learning. In short, engagement of the learner yields greater learning. The literature repeatedly contrasts active learning to passive exposure to new information; that is, sitting passively, listening, and taking notes (Felder and Brent, 2016; Tokuhama-Espinosa, 2014). Parents and Bible study leaders cannot toss out ideas and have them magically stick. As Coley states in *Teaching for Change*, "the learners' brains don't have Velcro!" (Coley, 2017). All learners—children, teens, and adults—need to have multiple experiences with new concepts beyond merely sitting and listening. Put another way, "the one doing the work is the one doing the learning" (Howard, 2015, p. 21). Well-known educator Robyn Jackson (2009) entitled her book on effective teaching, *Never Work Harder Than Your Students*, and asks this penetrating question of herself, "Was it more important that my students be quiet and cooperative, or was it more important that they actively engage with the material and learn to be critical thinkers and effective communicators?" (p. 93). Willis (2006) summarizes the value of engagement following an attention-grabbing introduction,

> To take advantage of their engaged state of mind, students should have the opportunities to interact with the information they need to learn. The goal is for them to actively discover, interpret, analyze, process, practice, and discuss the information so that it will move from working memory and be processed in the frontal lobe regions devoted to executive function. (p. 11)

Newton (2012) accurately balances the importance of engagement and experience with the parent/teacher's responsibility to provide God's Word as the fundamental building blocks.

> Teachers must build a platform of foundational facts and principles before students can build upon them to go deeper. On the other hand, just teaching facts, understandings, and concepts without interactive, experiential, and problem-solving learning experiences fails to help students understand how knowledge can be useful in life. (p. 166)

Love with all your heart, soul, and might (verse 5)

Edward J. Woods (2011) reminds us, "Deuteronomy has been aptly described as 'preached law'" (p. 31). It is the sermon series that Moses preached on the plains of Moab, directly east across the Jordan River from the Promised Land. Like preachers today, Moses began with the unchanging Word, the Torah God revealed at Sinai. He then explained the meanings of those words as they applied to the contemporary living dynamics the people were about to know in the Promised Land. No longer would they be forced to endure that barren, desperate wilderness (Deut. 8:2-3). Now their faith would be tested with fullness, abundance, and opportunity. They needed to prepare for this new reality! The message burning in Moses was, "When you get to the Promised Land, don't forget God! Keep living there by the words you were given here in the wilderness" (Deut. 8:11-20).

Much was at stake, yet Moses could not go with them. Israel was heading into territory that was completely alien to their prior experience. Everything would be different, except for the words of God. To paraphrase Neil Postman, Moses was passionate about sending the children of Israel as living messages into a time he would not live to see (first sentence in the Introduction to *The Disappearance of Childhood*, 1982).

As he preached, the prophet-priest reviewed the history of Israel and the revelation of God, especially the Ten Commandments (Deut. 5:1-21). First, he recited what was familiar. Then, he concluded with something fresh; he invested into Israel's memory banks an unforgettable, "cut to the chase" synopsis of all ten commands. If he brought the same message to one of today's congregations, he might say, "Here's the bottom line, people!"

Ve'Ahavta (You will love) the Lord your God! In Hebrew, the command to love is a straightforward call to decide, to choose, to prefer one over all others. The sense of this action-oriented, functional command is captured later in Deuteronomy when Moses pleads,

> I call heaven and earth to witness against you today, that I have set before you life and death, blessing and curse. Therefore choose life that you and your offspring may live, loving the Lord your God, obeying his voice and holding fast to him, for he is your life... (Deut. 30:19-20)

To love God is a deliberate, conscious decision to *shema*—that is, to obey—the God of Abraham, Isaac, and Jacob and thereby reject all other gods. To choose and exclusively follow God at all times is, of itself, compelling and revolutionary, but the incalculable depth of the command, which Jesus called the greatest of all, is conveyed even more by the "all" words that follow—with all your heart (*levav*), soul (*nephesh*), and strength (*me'odekah*).

Levav (heart and mind) is a one-word designation for all the inner dimensions of a person that God alone sees—one's attitudes, thinking processes, affections, and feelings. The command is to love the Lord with all that is deep within oneself. Greek translations of this command add the word *dianoia* (mind) to *cardia* (heart) in order to capture the full sense of the one Hebrew word *levav* (Matthew 22:37; Mark 12:30; Luke 10:27). Since *levav* includes the mind, Jews consider the diligent study of Torah to be the highest form of worship. How else could one love the Lord with all one's heart? (Ps. 1:1-3; 119:97-104).

Nephesh (soul and life) describes all the outer dimensions of a person— the aspects that other people see, hear, and experience. It is behavior, actions, work, and words. It even includes every breath, an essential evidence of life (Tverberg, 2006, pp. 33-34).

So far, Moses's "bottom line" summary is, "Love the Lord your God with all that is within you and with all that comes out of your life." How could a person love God more fully than that? Why does the greatest commandment not stop here?

Me'odekah is difficult to translate from Hebrew into any other language. Most commonly, of course, the word is rendered *might* or *strength*, but these fail to capture the forceful effort and passion imbedded in the word. Lois Tverberg (2006) says that trying to translate *me'odekah* "into one or two specific terms greatly diminishes its meaning" (p. 59).

"With all your *me'odekah*" literally means "with all your *very*" or "with all your *muchness*." The word imparts a superlative intensity that is difficult to convey linguistically. It is like saying, "Love the Lord your God with all your…oomph!" (Tverberg, 2006, p. 60).

So, after Moses reviewed the Ten Commandments in Deuteronomy 5, he passionately exclaimed, "Obey the Lord your God exclusively with all your innermost personal reflections; with all your outermost public expressions; and with all your efforts and exertions." No wonder Jesus called this the greatest commandment of all!

Reflective Practice

For more than a decade nearly every text on education has a chapter on and frequent mention of the concept of *reflective practice*. Just as Moses is exhorting parents "to have these words on your heart," to meditate on your heart's condition, contemporary educational literature urges teachers to diligently reflect on their instruction. Jackson (2009) argues that an educator with a master teacher mindset has the understanding that "meaningful reflection is critical to honing and refining your teaching craft" (p. 3). Tokuhama-Espinosa (2014) points out, "Modeling the behavior we hope to cultivate in our students requires that we be open to self-improvement ourselves" (p. 61). Hall and Simeral (2015), in *Teach, Reflect, Learn: Building Your Capacity for Success in the Classroom*, challenge those who lead children to practice this cycle continually:

- How aware am I of my students, the content, and the pedagogy?
- How intentionally do I plan and deliver all aspects of my teaching?
- How do I know whether my actions affect student learning?
- How effectively do I respond to the results of ongoing assessments? (p. 39)

You shall teach them diligently to your children, and shall talk of them (verses 6-7a)

To some, *teach* and *talk* may sound like two ways of saying the same thing. That is not the case in this passage. *Teach* cannot be separated from the qualifier before it in verse 6: *These words that I command you today shall be on your heart.*

Gary Newton (2012) writes, "When Moses explains next that 'these words that I am giving you today are to be in your heart,' he used the term *heart* not in order to distinguish it from *soul* and *strength* but rather to emphasize that our love for God should be embedded at the core of our being. *Heart* was understood to be the deepest and most comprehensive term for everything we are and all that we have" (p. 19).

This points to the essence of Hebrew pedagogy. Common sense indicates it is also the most effective way to educate. Simply stated, the pedagogy says, "First do, then talk."

Verses 5-7 progress from loving God fervently (verse 5) to living His commandments from the inside out (verse 6) with such repetitive consistency that the truth pierces the conscience and consciousness of your children. And after that, "talk" (verse 7).

The word for *teach* in verse 7 is not *lamad*, which is the usual root used in Deuteronomy (e.g., Deut. 4:1 and 5:1). *Teach* in verse 7 is like *heart* in verse 5 in that it is one Hebrew word that requires at least two in English to capture its nuances. The basic root of the word in verse 7 is *shinan*, which means *repeat* (as in Prov. 17:9). But in verse 7, the same root is rendered as a special kind of repetition—that which whets or sharpens. (The same word is used again in Deuteronomy 32:41). So, this word, translated *teach*, expresses repetitive instruction that is also sharp and incisive, piercing through to the desired results (Gesenius, 1907, pp. 1041-42). What a powerful picture! In English, this one word is usually translated, *teach diligently.*

A holistic look at the Deuteronomy 6 passage demands that *diligent teaching* be understood as that which goes *beyond words*. At minimum, it is the purposeful repetition of life's most important lessons via active and honest personal example. In this educational design, children experience commandments before they hear them. This pedagogy is incisive and effective because children are already more inclined to imitate behaviors than they are to listen to lectures.

Connecting to Schema

When the learner encounters new information, he asks, "Where do I put this, or do I have to establish a new bucket?" Research says that greater learning takes place when new information is attached to prior learning and experiences. Ambrose, Bridges, DiPietro, Lovett, and Norman (2010) explains, "The extent to which students are able to draw on prior knowledge to effectively construct new knowledge depends on the nature of their prior knowledge, as well as the instructor's ability to harness it" (p. 15). Another term for prior learning is *schema* (Marazano, 2007). Neurologist and educator Judy Willis (2006) describes how new information is stored and becomes part of long-term memory: "The more times one repeats an action or recalls the information, the more dendrites sprout on neurons to connect new memories to old, and the more efficient the brain becomes in its ability to retrieve that memory or repeat that action" (p. 8). This is a 21st century expression of the diligent teaching that leads to the sharpening described above.

In recommending how to design the introduction of a lesson, Rollins (2017) magnificently summarizes the need for connection to prior learning and transitions to the next educational concept:

> "Our mission is to identify and develop prior knowledge for new learning, articulate our new learning target, establish relevance, and pique intellectual curiosity. These activities are often collaborative, thought-provoking, and designed to further student success in the lesson" (p. 42).

Elaboration

Elaboration is the educational term for the process of expressing new information in the learner's own words (Schwartz, Tsang, & Blair, 2016). Research states that when the learner is able to do that, then greater learning and memory retention take place. "Elaboration is the process of giving new material meaning by expressing it in your own words and connecting it with what you already know. If you practice elaboration, there's no known limit to what you can learn" (Brown, Roediger, & McDaniel, 2014, p. 5).

In a recent article on developing the intellectual skill of argumentation, Ehrenworth (2017) suggests teachers "consider starting with talk" (p. 36), with the ultimate goal of developing students' logic and reasoning skills. The researcher concludes, "In fact, one of the fastest ways to raise the level of students' argument writing is to raise the level of their talk—their argument discourse" (p. 36).

In a related discussion Hunter (2015) has a chapter entitled, "Helping Parents Dive Deep," which discusses a systematic approach to moving conversations from superficial topics about routine events, to deeper issues about their children's feelings and emotions, to a third level of meaningful depth. At the third level, conversations of real influence occur (pp. 93-102).

In our day, just as it was for Moses' contemporaries, talking about new ideas and rehearsing their meaning present learners with opportunities to re-state the concept and not just parrot back words they heard in an earlier teaching episode. Unlike the teaching environment for Moses, our students frequently use some type of note-taking process, whether with paper/pencil or digital means. A popular technique for elaboration in a more formal lecture setting is for the presenter to pause and allow time for students to review their notes, summarize the major ideas in their own words, and then share the words with a peer or the instructor to check for accuracy.

Authentic Work Products

Time and again research has supported the motivational power and effectiveness of presenting new information the learner views as authentic, that is, directly meaningful to his life and context (Ambrose et al., 2010). By contrast, exposing learners to new concepts they do not perceive as meaningful to their lives *decreases* the likelihood of deep learning and long-term retention.

If our goal is to increase learner motivation, Ambrose et al. (2010) challenges us to "Assign problems and tasks that allow students to vividly and concretely see the relevance and value of otherwise abstract concepts and theories" (p. 83). The following characteristics of authentic learning reflect the spirit and substance of verses 6-7:

1. Activity that involves real-world problems, mimics the work of professionals; the activity involves presentation of findings to audiences beyond the classroom.
2. Use of open-ended inquiry, thinking skills, and metacognition.
3. Students engage in discourse and social learning in a community of learners. (Rule,   2006, p. 1-10)

When you sit in your house (verse 7b)

In *Character Driven College Preparation: The Mission and Method of the University-Model® School,* Turner (2017) traces the educational progression of Deuteronomy 6. After God inspires through Moses the original statement of the greatest commandment (verse 5), he then reveals his grandest strategy for imparting the love of Him from generation to generation. First, the commandments are to be lived from the heart in daily life (verse 6). The modeling of godliness through personal example gives children real and repeated experiences in the love of God.

Parents in particular are charged to talk about the commandments with their children in four designated "classrooms" (Turner, 2017, pp. 10-12). They are not physical classrooms, of course, but daily occasions of life experience. Those classrooms are "when you sit in your house, when you walk by the way, when you lie down, and when you rise up." Parents are uniquely in position to talk with their children in those four settings.

In today's culture, the four "classrooms" are often considered to be down times or in-between times—certainly not the main events in a day. For instance, to sit in one's house implies relaxation, relative inactivity, and recovery from the pace of the marketplace. "Walking by the way" today is more likely to be "commuting in the car," but commuting is not the goal. Arriving is. Likewise, "lying down" at bedtime and "rising up" at breakfast are not ends in themselves. They are means to the ends that are considered much more important.

Why would the four "classrooms" be identified as key times for parents to talk with their children about God's love and commandments? Why are these down times to be treated as prime times? In all four venues, a parent's guard is down, the "mask" is off, and the parents consciously or unconsciously exercise their personal preferences, choices, beliefs, and values in full view of the children. Positive or negative, constructive or destructive, these values are caught and taught in the informal arenas of everyday life. Through their attitudes, actions, direct instructions, and casual conversations, the parents impart a framework that children will work within to organize experiences, attribute worth, and apply knowledge.

When children experience parents who really do "have the commandments in their hearts," then faith in God becomes bigger than any religious activity or event. Faith becomes a life-giving love for one another and for the world around us.

Practice That Is Spaced

In the *four classrooms* described above, new material is taught and new concepts are rehearsed throughout the day as opposed to concentrated sessions with a rigid time schedule. This instructional approach is called *spaced practice* as opposed to *massed practice* (Lang, 2016, p. 66).

A growing body of research about how we learn flies in the face of traditional methods associated with rote memorization and massed practice. The act of remembering, including the struggle to recall, actually strengthens the connections between new and previously learned information, which leads to stronger retention of the new ideas.

> "When we engage in massed learning exercises, focusing on one set of content repeatedly, we never have to access the learned material from the deeper recesses of our long-term memory. By contrast, if we use spaced learning to allow some time for the forgetting of the material to set in, we are forced to draw material from our longer-term memory when we return to it." (Lang, 2016, pp. 66-67)

Practice That Is Interleaved

Research reveals that practice needs to be both *spaced* and *interleaved*—that is practice needs to include different activities interspersed with the particular skill the learner is focused on. Simply put, repeating the same drill over and over is not the most effective way to learn something. It is rather to concentrate on a new idea and then move on to a related topic before that idea has been mastered, and then returning to the first idea, and then perhaps adding a third one (Lang, 2016, p. 68). As with spaced practice, interleaving stretches students by challenging them to recall information. Well-known educational consultant Marianne Weimer (2017) concludes, "The more often they find it, go back to it, review it, and connect it with what they already know, the more likely they are to understand and remember it" (p. 2).

Practice That Is Varied

The learner needs to be exposed to a variety of learning experiences. One need only examine the multiple approaches that successful coaches employ to reinforce new skills and team plays, or the variety of approaches used by chorus and band directors in rehearsals. The authors of *Make It Stick* summarize this discussion by stating, "Practice that's spaced out, interleaved with other learning, and varied produces better mastery, longer retention, and more versatility. But these benefits come at a price: when practice is spaced, interleaved and varied, it requires more effort" (Brown, Roediger, and McDaniel, 2014, p. 47).

When you walk by the way (verse 7b)

The word for *way* in this phrase of verse 7 is *darakh*. It is derived from the verb *to tread* and carries extraordinary educational connotations. First, there are the physical attributes of a *way* or *path* in ancient times. Long before there were chariots or wagons, a *way* was a well-worn footpath for humans and animals born of the necessity for water. One was not wise to trek his own random path across the land according to his preference. *Ways* were life-giving maps, etched in the landscape, assuring the traveler that the road was passable and survivable. The tests of time had confirmed that water was available in the form of wells, cisterns, springs, or small streams. A *darakh*, therefore, was a proven pathway to walk with a child and talk about God's covenant commands.

In Scripture, the root of *darakh* appears over 750 times, often in the theological sense. In Exodus 33:13, Moses cried out to the Lord, "If I have found favor in your sight, please show me now your *ways*." In Isaiah 55:8, God said to the nation, "My *ways* are not your *ways*" (Lowin, p. 29). In Psalm 143:8, David prays, "Make me know the *way* I should go." The physical features of an ancient way beautifully illustrate the Proverbs 3:5-6 principle: "Do not lean on your own understanding. In all your *ways* acknowledge him." Finally, in Jeremiah 6:16, the prophet appeals, "Stand by the *roads* and look, and ask for the ancient paths, where the good *way* is; and walk in it, and find rest for your souls."

In modern Hebrew, *darakh* is still the root of travel-related words like sidewalk, passport, odometer, and road (Lowin, 1995, p. 30). It is actually the case in Israel today that ancient ways, which began as simple footpaths millennia ago are now well-established, paved, and permanent thoroughfares.

Establishing Patterns of Thinking

Current mind, brain, and education research clearly establishes how "the way" can become part of the mental framework of your child as he/she turns a mental footpath into a country road, which can become a neighborhood street, then a parkway, and finally a freeway. Once again, the coaching in Deuteronomy is magnificently supported by modern educators. In a discussion on "patterns are paths for memories to follow," Willis (2006) explains,

> Education is about increasing the patterns that students can use, recognize, and communicate. As the ability to see and work with patterns expands, the executive functions are enhanced. Whenever new material is presented in such a way that students see relationships, they generate greater brain cell activity….and achieve more successful long-term memory storage and retrieval. (p. 15)

Bind them as a sign and as frontlets (verse 8)

These exact phrases in verse 8 with the words *oth* (sign) and *totaphoth* (frontlets or headbands) are also used in Exodus 13:16 where, as in Deuteronomy 6, the teaching of future generations looms large. In the Exodus passage, fathers are enjoined to faithfully teach their sons that all firstborn males (human and livestock alike) belong to the Lord; therefore, they are to be sacrificed or redeemed with a substitute (Ex. 13:1-2, 11-13). This consecration of the firstborn was a public act in full view of the children. And "when" the sons asked why, the fathers were instructed to reply,

By a strong hand the Lord brought us out of Egypt, from the house of slavery. For when Pharaoh stubbornly refused to let us go, the Lord killed all the firstborn in the land of Egypt...Therefore I sacrifice to the Lord all the males that first open the womb, but all the firstborn of my sons I redeem. (Ex. 13:14b-15)

According to the next verse, there is a teaching tandem of visible example followed by verbal explanation. "And it shall be for a token upon thine hand, and for frontlets between thine eyes" (Ex. 13:16, KJV). The process itself is designed to wrap a lesson around a son's conscious awareness so he never forgets what God did to redeem his fathers.

In Deuteronomy 6:8, the context is similar. Moses commands the people to love the Lord and make sure every generation thereafter does the same. He exhorts them to 1) have the *devarim* (words) in their hearts, 2) visibly act them out (obey them) in daily life, and 3) verbally repeat them with sharp precision to the children and grandchildren (Deut. 6:6-7). As in Exodus 13, the next verse says, "You shall bind them as a sign (*oth*) on your hand, and they shall be as frontlets (*totaphoth*) between your eyes." This manner of instruction (first do, then talk) etches God's commandments into children's memory banks via multi-sensory exposure (seeing, hearing, and experiencing).

Centuries after Moses spoke these words (Gesenius, 1907, p. 378), the rabbis began to apply meticulous guidelines for daily prayers, based on verse 8, that included the physical tying of Scripture portions to the hands and foreheads in literal obedience (see also Deut. 11:18-21; Prov. 1:9; 3:3; 6:21; 7:3). The secondary practices of donning *tefillin* (the word means prayers) or *phylacteries* were physical repetitions (at least three times daily) intended to draw attention to repeating the primary behaviors commanded in the passage—to live out God's commandments from the heart and then speak them to children as a normal part of daily life.

Jesus chastised the Pharisees, not because they put on phylacteries, but because they had turned the practices into selfish ends in themselves, neglecting the weightier matters of the Torah (Matt. 23:2-7, 23).

Chunking

The practice of storing bits of the Torah in phylacteries beautifully illustrates the educational concept of chunking. Felder and Brent (2016) describe the research behind the cognitive processing theory that is consistent with the practice described in verse 8. "When people's cognitive load at a given time exceeds the processing capacity of their working memory, their brain is in a state of *cognitive overload*, and they will be unable to process new incoming information without losing information already present in working memory" (p. 92). Solution: *chunking*, dividing the material into units that the brain can retain. For example, in our everyday transactions social security numbers, credit card numbers, and ten-digit phone numbers are all printed in chunks.

Reflection

Planning ahead to review Scripture allows the disciple to reflect on both its meaning and his progress toward applying it. "Reflection is a form of retrieval practice (What happened? What did I do? How did it work out?), enhanced with elaboration (What would I do differently next time?)" (Brown, Roediger, and McDaniel, 2014, p. 66).

Write them on your door posts and your gates (verse 9)

To obey this command literally, the rabbis again prescribed that a follower of Torah should roll up a small written copy of the *Shema*, physically insert it into a small cylinder or box called a *mezuzah* and attach it to the doorpost of a home or business. As with phylacteries, the point was not so much to remember the container. It was the commandments inside that mattered. Reaching up to touch the *mezuzah* was a consistent reminder to do the words written therein and, having done them, to talk of them faithfully.

Imagine a wife asking her husband, "Do you love me?" The husband replies, "Of course I do, honey, and here's proof: I'm wearing this wedding ring!" This analogy speaks for itself. A wedding ring is only as meaningful as the actions of consistent, genuine love it represents and inspires. By the same token, the *mezuzah* on the door post is only as good as the active obedience to God it calls forth.

But when a believer touches that container on the doorpost and, as a result, remembers and worships the Lord, how precious does that *mezuzah* become?

Durable Learning

Catching your child's attention with these visual aids, at the doorposts and your gates, is coaching them "coming and going." These multiple avenues of experience lead to deeper, more durable learning. An often-cited statement is "Cells that fire together wire together" (Willis, 2006, 7). "Knowledge is more durable if it's deeply entrenched, meaning that you have firmly and thoroughly comprehended a concept, it has practical importance or keen emotional weight in your life, and it is connected with other knowledge that you hold" (Brown, Roediger, & McDaniel, 2014, p. 77).

Implications

A multitude of articles and books exist on the topic of "losing the next generation." Some are scholarly, most are not. Christian Smith (2009), a Harvard-trained sociologist and researcher, has done extensive data collection on teens' spiritual development and reached this conclusion about the impact of four factors in a teen's life: "The combination of the teenager's parental religion, importance of faith, of prayer, and of scripture reading makes an enormous substantive difference in religious outcomes during emerging adulthood" (p. 220). These factors appear to influence durable learning and a sustained faith. Having established the magnitude of the responsibility to teach our children and grand-children, the authors of this article present these implications:

1) Scripture reminds both parents and ministry leaders of the significance of their roles in training/discipling the next generation. The powerful concepts embedded in each verse in Deuteronomy 6 are as vitally important in the 21st century as they were to Moses and his contemporaries.

2) Curriculum writers are encouraged to take note of the expanded understanding of instructional techniques that are taught in the passage. It's not enough to convince parents and leaders that it is important to train

children at home and church, but how they go about it is a significant part of the teaching in this passage. The mind, brain, and education research points to thoughtfully structured practice using a variety of learning modalities and to skillfully connecting new ideas to the learner's context and prior learning—all of these instructional concepts presented in the focal passage.

3) While parents should continue to prepare for a specific time to teach their children each day (following a meal, evening family time, before bed), one of the principles revealed in this study is the importance of introducing new ideas, reinforcing them, and reviewing them with their children throughout the day, not just at a single time. The truths of God's Word are best remembered when they are presented periodically in both planned and spontaneous ways, in the four classrooms mentioned by Moses.

4) Social media and technology need not be the enemy in current approaches to training children. An occasional reminder ("when you walk by the way"), a visual representation ("on your doorpost"), and a chance for elaboration ("talk about this") by way of mobile devices can be present-day phylacteries and gateposts that expand parents' influence beyond their homes during busy days and hectic seasons.

It is our prayer that you will love the Lord with "all your very" and will teach your children "with all your oomph!"

References

Ambrose, S. A., Bridges, M. W., DiPietro, M., Lovett, M. C., & Norman, M. K. (2010). *How learning works: Seven research-based principles for smart teaching*. The Jossey-Bass Higher and Adult Education Series. San Francisco, CA: Jossey-Bass.

Bain, K. (2004). *What the best college teachers do*. Cambridge, MA: Harvard University Press.

Brown, P. C., Roediger, III, H. L., & McDaniel, M. A. (2014). *Make it stick: The science of successful learning*. Cambridge, MA: Belknap Press of Harvard University Press.

Carey, B. (2015). *How we learn: The surprising truth about when, where, and why it happens*. New York, NY: Random House.

Coley, K. (2017). *Teaching for change: Eight keys for transformational Bible study with teens*. Nashville, TN: Randall House.

Ehrenworth, M. (2017). Why argue? *Educational Leadership, 74*(5), 35-40.

Felder, R. M., & Brent, R. (2016). *Teaching and learning STEM: A practical guide*. San Francisco, CA: Jossey-Bass.

Gesenius, W. (1907). *A Hebrew and English lexicon of the Old Testament*. F. Brown, S. R. Driver, & C. A. Briggs (Eds.), and E. Robinson (Trans.). Oxford: Clarendon Press.

Hall, P., & Simeral, A. (2015). *Teach reflect learn: Building your capacity for success in the classroom*. Alexandria, VA: ASCD.

Hendricks, H. C., & William, D. (1991). *Living by the Book*. Chicago, IL: Moody Press.

The Holy Bible, English Standard Version. (2001). Wheaton, IL: Crossway Bibles, A Division of Good News Publishers.

Howard, J. R. (2015). *Discussion in the college classroom: Getting your students engaged and participating in person and online*. San Francisco, CA: Jossey-Bass.

Hunter, R., Jr. (2015). *The DNA of D6: Building blocks of generational discipleship*. Nashville, TN: Randall House.

Jackson, R. R. (2009). *Never work harder than your students: And other principles of great teaching*. Alexandria, VA: ASCD.

Lang, J. M. (2016). *Small teaching: Everyday lessons from the science of learning*. San Francisco, CA: Jossey-Bass.

Lowin, J. (1995). *Hebrewspeak: An insider's guide to the way Jews think*. Northvale, NJ: Jason Aronson Inc.

Marzano, R. J. (2007). *The art and science of teaching: A comprehensive framework for effective instruction*. Alexandria, VA: Association for Supervision and Curriculum Development.

Newton, G. (2012). *Heart-deep teaching: Engaging students for transformed lives*. Nashville, TN: B&H.

Postman, N. (1982). *The disappearance of childhood*. New York, NY: Delacorte Press.

Rollins, S. P. (2017). *Teaching in the fast lane: How to create active learning experiences*. Alexandria, VA: ASCD.

Rule, A. (2006). Editorial: The components of authentic learning. *Journal of Authentic Learning, 3*(1), 1-10.

Schwartz, D. L., Tsang, J. M., & Blair, K. P. (2016). *The ABCs of how we learn: 26 scientifically proven approaches, how they work, and when to use them.* New York, NY: W.W. Norton.

Smith, C. (with Snell, P.). (2009). *Souls in transition: The religious and spiritual lives of emerging adults.* New York, NY: Oxford University Press.

Tokuhama-Espinosa, T. (2011). *Mind, brain, and education science: A comprehensive guide to the new brain-based teaching.* New York, NY: W. W. Norton.

Tokuhama-Espinosa, T. (2014). *Making classrooms better: 50 practical applications of mind, brain, and education science.* New York, NY: W. W. Norton.

Turner, J. W., Jr. (2017). *Character driven college preparation: The mission and method of the University-Model® school.* Midlothian, TX: NAUMS, Inc.

Tverberg, L. (with Okkema, B.). (2006). Listening to the language of the Bible: Hearing it through Jesus' ears. Holland, MI: En-Gedi Resource Center.

Vine, W. E. (1984). *Vine's complete expository dictionary of Old and New Testament words.* Nashville, TN: Thomas Nelson.

Weimer, M. (2017, January). Interleaving: An evidence-based study strategy. *Faculty Focus.* Retrieved from https://www.facultyfocus.com/articles/teaching-professor-blog/interleaving-evidence-based-study-strategy/.

Willis, J. (2006). *Research-based strategies to ignite student learning: Insights from a neurologist and classroom teacher.* Alexandria, VA: ASCD.

Wilson, D., & Conyers, M. (2013). *Five big ideas for effective teaching: Connecting mind, brain, and education research to classroom practice.* New York, NY: Teachers College Press.

Wilson, M. R. (1989). *Our father Abraham: Jewish roots of the Christian faith.* Grand Rapids, MI: William B. Eerdmans.

Woods, E. J. (2011). Deuteronomy: An introduction and commentary. In D. Firth (Ed.), *Tyndale Old Testament Commentaries* (Vol. 5). Downers Grove, IL: InterVarsity Press.

Author Biographies

Kenneth S. Coley, Ed.D. leads the Doctor of Education Program at Southeastern Baptist Theological Seminary in Wake Forest, North Carolina. His most recent book is *Teaching for Change* (2017), published by Randall House.

John William Turner, Jr., D.Min., is Executive Director of Father's House Educational Foundation in Glen Rose, Texas and Family Ministry Coordinator of the National Association of University-Model® Schools in Midlothian, Texas. His most recent book is *Character Driven College Preparation: The Mission and Method of the University-Model® School* (2017) published by NAUMS, Inc.

Accessible Gospel and the Inclusive Leader: The Good Shepherd Discourse and the Disability-Effective Pastor

Dr. Chris Hulshof

In her book, *Same Lake, Different Boat*, Stephanie Hubach (2006) tells the story of a friend who brought her disabled son to a small-town hospital emergency room. This child had suffered a seizure and injured his mouth and tongue. He was in need of immediate help. The emergency room physician looked over the child and determined there was nothing he could do. It was beyond his experience and expertise. However, he did not consult other staff or doctors. He did not even propose treatment at another hospital. He simply sent the mother and her son on their way. This lack of concern for proper healthcare resulted in the boy needing weeks of medical treatment in a different hospital for his damaged tongue and mouth. Hubach summarizes her response to this story:

> When I first heard this tale, a myriad of emotions swelled up within me. The hospital's response—so obviously inappropriate and inhumane—engendered intense feelings of disbelief and indignation. "Isn't a hospital supposed to be a refuge of hospitality, a place of welcoming care for everyone in need of medical attention? How could anyone possibly do that to another human being in such apparent need?" And then it struck me: This story is an ugly but accurate parable of what we do—at times—in the church. Sometimes we forget that the church is not a country club for members but a hospital for sinners of all different stripes, with all different types of needs. And when we forget this, our response

will probably be to shut the door: "Members Only. We can't deal with this." (p. 152)

Hubach's observation is correct with regard to those who are disabled. It is still too commonplace for Christians who suffer from impairment to find themselves marginalized within the church.

This reality runs counter to the inclination and design of God. The Scriptures establish God's compassion for the disabled as well as His desire for their inclusion in the household of faith. The Old Testament demonstrates this compassion and desire through narrative and instruction (e.g., Leviticus 21:17-23; 2 Samuel 9). In the New Testament, the life and teaching of Jesus Christ avows His Father's position on disabilities. This affirmation is primarily evidenced through His numerous encounters with the disabled. Furthermore, the apostles practiced the compassion and inclusion they learned from Jesus. One example of their practice is Peter's interaction with the lame man in Acts 3:1-10. This biblical and theological trajectory for disabilities provides the impetus for the contemporary church to be a standard bearer of compassion and inclusion.

Sadly, church leaders have been ill-prepared for a ministry that is cognizant of those with disabilities who are part of their congregation. This problematic oversight creates an ecclesiastical climate where leaders must self-educate on disabilities, disability ministry, and disability-effective leadership. Resources that address these concerns from a biblical perspective are scant. At best, the church pastor must investigate educational offerings on disability and attempt to modify the material so it is suitable both personally and congregationally. At worst, the church leader deems the situation as awkward and the risk of embarrassment greater than the reward of potential inclusion. Thus, the marginalization of the disabled and the continued Country Club mentality persist within his church.

The literary unit of John 9:1—10:21 details Jesus's encounter first with a blind man and then with the religious leaders. This encounter leads to His discourse on the good shepherd. The good shepherd discourse underscores four relational qualities that are evident in the disability-effective pastor. In order to see these four qualities, one must first recognize an error present in most disability studies related to John 9. This error is one of context. It understands John 10:1-21 as a speech that takes place sometime after the healing of the blind man and apart from the presence of the religious leaders. Once the proper connection between John 9 and 10 is established, a bridge between disabilities and the relational qualities of the disability-effective pastor is formed.

Common Studies of Disability and John 9

A quick review of most biblical literature on disability or disability ministry will predictably include space dedicated to the healing of the blind man in John 9 (e.g., Beates, 2012; Block, 2002; Brock & Swinton, 2012; Eiesland & Saliers, 1998; Yong, 2011). It would seem that the disciples theological question about the connection of sin and disability is one of the catalysts for the scrutiny this chapter receives. A second possible reason for its continued use in biblical discussions on disability is related to the way a disabled man goes from no faith to a follower of Christ. Thus, it makes for an easy methodology of evangelism and discipleship with regard to the disabled. A third apparent reason for the inclusion of the healing in John 9 in most biblical discussions on disability is the contrast it presents to the healing in John 5. In John 9, the man born blind responds positively to the healing and becomes a follower of Jesus. The healing story in John 5 presents the opposite situation. Upon recognition of his healer, the once-lame man reports to the religious leaders who his healer was instead of becoming a follower of Jesus.

Connecting John 9 and John 10: Another Way of Investigating the Healing of the Blind Man in John 9

One area is often neglected in disability related studies of John 9. This area is the intended connection between John 9 and John 10. Contextually, the literary unit runs from John 9:1 through to John 10:21. Thus, following the healing of the blind man, Jesus moves to discuss His role as the Good Shepherd and how it is contrasted to the role occupied by the religious leaders. Their actions against the once-blind man spur this comparison. This connection has grand implications for the disability-effective pastor or church leader. For Jesus, leaders who lack the divine compassion and sympathy for the once-blind man give evidence they are not true shepherds. Further, the inability of these leaders to recognize this divine compassion and mercy in Jesus also adds to this indictment.

Comfort and Hawley (2007) state that John 10:1-21 is a carryover of Christ's comments to the Pharisees. The words of Jesus address the way these religious leaders have treated the once-blind man. They have banished him from Judaism in general and the synagogue in particular. Thus, Jesus is portraying this man as anyone who leaves Judaism in order to follow Jesus. They are sheep following their Shepherd (p. 137). Burge (2000) also takes this position. He argues that John 10:1-21 is a continuation of John 9, since no new audience is assumed, and John 10:21 refers to the blind man's healing. He summarizes that these opening verses demonstrate that the once-blind man does not follow the Pharisees because he does not recognize their voice. Like a sheep, this man knows the voice of the True Shepherd, and he follows Him rather than the false shepherds or Pharisees. Burge notes that John 10:1-21 serves to severely critique the failed leadership of the Pharisees in John 9 (p. 286).

For Morris (1995), the connection between John 9 and John 10 is evident in the opening words of "I assure you" or "Truly, Truly, I say to you" (ESV). Morris stresses that this phrase is not used elsewhere to begin a discourse. Rather, it is a technique used to follow up a previous teaching and serves as a connector between the forthcoming explanation and the prior instruction (p. 446).

Köstenberger (2004) understands this event in a way that ought to bring about a foreboding sense to the discerning reader. He writes,

> Chapter 10 follows chapter 9 without transition (see also 10:21); thus, Jesus's audiences are likely the same. Jesus's healing of the blind man had led to the man's expulsion from the local synagogue, an act viewed by Jesus as an arrogant assertion of usurped authority that called for further comment. For the Pharisees were not only blind themselves (9:40-41); they were also "blind guides" (cf. Matt. 23:16, 24) who led astray those entrusted to their care. The dark backdrop of Jesus's good shepherd discourse is therefore the blatant irresponsibility of the Jewish religious leaders. (p. 298)

Rhodes (2016) astutely notes the sensory connection that links John 10 to John 9. He indicates that Jesus switches from visual to aural imagery in order to explain to the Pharisees that the voice of the true shepherd is one that the sheep hear and follow. Further, Rhodes believes that the sheep Jesus has in mind are both those in the present context, as well as all subsequent listeners. Thus, like the blind man, those who follow Jesus today have not seen Him but have heard and responded to His voice as it is heard throughout the Scriptures (p. 65).

This connection between John 9 and John 10 is frequently missed in disability studies. The narrowed focus for disability research in John 9 concentrates on the blind man and his healing. This limitation causes the majority of material to be concentrated on the question of sin, the contrast with John 5, or an assumed pattern of discipleship. Studies that stop at the end of John 9 rather than continuing through into John 10 inevitably pay little attention to the discourse of Jesus throughout these two chapters. When these two chapters are viewed Christologically, rather than anthropomorphically, it draws attention to the good shepherd discourse and the character of the good shepherd. Further, it proposes four relational qualities that the good shepherd possess. Each of these qualities, when modeled by a pastor or church leader, demonstrate what disability-effective ministry looks like.

The Good Shepherd Discourse:
Who is the true shepherd and who is a false shepherd?

The ongoing dialogue between Jesus, the once-blind man, and the religious leaders culminates in the man becoming a follower of Jesus and to his expulsion from the synagogue. As a result of this dismissal, Jesus addresses the way that the Pharisees have reacted to him, the once-blind man's healing, and his ensuing declaration about Jesus (John 10:1-19). Using a common cultural image combined with the prophetic words of Ezekiel, Jesus identifies Himself as the Good Shepherd while the religious leaders are more like the evil shepherds spoken of in Ezekiel 34. This profound illustration tells us much about the work of God that Jesus knows He and His disciples need to accomplish. However, Jesus also mixes the metaphor up in this section as well. He calls Himself the door or the gate to the sheep pen. This metaphor allows Him to juxtapose His character with those He considers thieves and robbers. Both the image of the good shepherd and the door to the sheep pen are images worth exploring because of the implications each of these have for disability ministry.

In order to understand an image that can easily be lost in a non-agrarian culture, a short summary of the life of a shepherd is necessary. Sproul (2009) adequately summarizes the routine of a shepherd. He comments,

> In those days, there was one large, central pen, or sheepfold, in a given community, and at the end of the day people brought their small individual flocks and led them into the big sheepfold. With their combined resources, they paid a gatekeeper, and it was his job to stay with the sheep during the night. In the morning, the gatekeeper opened the gate to those who were truly shepherds, whose sheep were enclosed in the sheepfold. The shepherds entered by the door, for they had every right to do so—the sheep were theirs and the gatekeeper was their paid servant. When a shepherd entered the sheepfold, the sheep of all the local flocks were mixed, but he began to call, and his sheep recognized his voice and came to him. In fact, a good shepherd was so intimately involved with the care and the nurture of his sheep that he had names for them, and he would call them by name. His sheep followed him out because they knew him. (p. 187)

The information provided in this succinct description sheds valuable light on the metaphor employed by Jesus. As the Shepherd, He enters the sheep fold appropriately, He knows His sheep, He calls His sheep, He leads them out, and they follow Him because they know His voice. Each of these elements is represented in the work God has sent Jesus to do (John 9:4-5). This job description of a shepherd also serves as points of condemnation for the Pharisees. Jesus identifies them as the false shepherds.

Four Relational Qualities of the Good Shepherd

In Jesus's illustration, the bond described between the shepherd and his sheep draws attention to four relational qualities that exist between the master and his flock. The first section of John 10:1-21 points to the relational qualities of intimacy and trust (John 10:1-6). The second section addresses the relational quality of accessibility (John 10:7-10). Finally, the third section speaks to the relational quality of sacrifice (John 10:11-21).

Intimacy

Gangel (2000) hints that the active verbs of opens, listen, calls, and leads, of John 10:3 are important to understanding the relationship between the shepherd and his sheep. Specifically, he believes these four words are indicative of the affection that exists between them. Supporting this claim, Gangel emphasizes that the shepherd calls his sheep by name. His call is not simply a singular address to the whole flock. Further, Gangel notes that John also uses the phrase "by name" in his third epistle where he tells Gaius, "The friends send you greetings. Greet the friends by name" (3 John 14) (pp. 195-196). Contextually then, there is a friendly and affectionate connotation to the way the shepherd calls his own sheep. He is not simply addressing them as a group. Instead, knowing each of his sheep individually, he calls them by name.

Wilson (1906) further develops this imagery pointing to John 10:3 and revealing that,

> "The shepherds often give names to their sheep. These names are descriptive of some trait or characteristic of the animal, as Long-ears, White-nose, Speckled, and so forth. Not unfrequently the sheep get to know their names and will answer to them when called." (p.165)

More recently, Keener (2003) also demonstrates that shepherds individually named and called their sheep by those names. He notes that shepherds preferred a shorter name like "snowy" since this allowed for quickly calling the animals. Additionally, names were often selected based on shape, color, or peculiarities. This naming practice is indicative of familiarity and affection (p. 805).

While there may be some danger in blurring the illustrative lines between this shepherding practice and the present-day domestication of cats and dogs. Perhaps it may be helpful though, since most modern North American Christians have little familiarity with shepherding. When one brings home a cat or a dog one of the first tasks is to select a suitable name. The naming of the animal only increases the level of affection between the owner and that cat or dog. This is the type of affection Jesus is trying to impress upon the religious leaders and all who are overhearing this discussion with this shepherd and sheep imagery. There is an intimacy between the shepherd and his sheep. This human/animal affection is akin to the type of affection the modern human beings have for their pets. Köstenberger (2004) nicely summarizes the meaning of Jesus's metaphor when he writes, "This intimacy of shepherd and his flock provides a beautiful illustration of the trust, familiarity, and bond existing between Jesus and his followers" (p. 302).

The relational quality of intimacy challenges how well the pastor or church leader knows the members of his congregation. It is easy for those who are disabled to slip in and out of weekly worship and beyond any comradery with the pastor. While their disability may make them highly visible they exist in an almost invisible manner to the church leader. Youth pastors routinely get to know their youth group through athletic events, high school plays, or band concerts. However, a disabled student might not participate in these types of activities. Their lack of participation in common high school activities can lead to invisibility within the youth group. Consequently, a wise youth pastor will look for opportunities to get to know the disabled student in areas where he or she excels or finds enjoyment.

Trust

A second important relational quality is mentioned by Köstenberger in the previous section. It is the relational quality of trust. Ridderbos (1997) recognizes a level of trust that exists between the shepherd and the sheep. When the sheep hear the shepherd's voice their ears perk up. They become attentive as he calls them by their familiar names. They follow him as he leads them out. For the shepherd, he only moves on once he is sure every one of his sheep have left the fold. Then and only then, does he place himself in front of them as he leads them to pasture. The shepherd is familiar to the sheep and the sheep are familiar to the shepherd (p. 355).

It is this connection to the voice of the shepherd that shows the trust the sheep have in the shepherd. Carson (1991) suggests that it is simply because the sheep know the shepherd's voice that they follow him. Their following from familiarity stands against their inattentiveness to the voice of a stranger. They do not follow the stranger, because they do not recognize his voice (p. 383). This understanding is also taken by Haenchen (1984) when he states, "That the sheep follow him because they recognize his voice shows that they trust him" (p. 47). Thus, the trust connection between the sheep and the shepherd is related to their familiarity to his voice. The shepherd recognizes each one of them as his own. However, the inverse is also true, the sheep are so in tuned to the voice of the shepherd that they obediently come and follow when they hear his voice. When another voice appeals for them to follow him as their shepherd, the sheep do not recognize the voice and will not trust that shepherd.

Interestingly, Tenney (1964) moves the issue of trust beyond the aural to the experiential. He notes that the shepherd has the right to enter the fold at any time and that he commands the attention of the sheep. Additionally, the sheep follow him because they trust his leadership. Tenney makes this assumption as a means of connecting the shepherd of John 10:1-6 to the Good Shepherd of John 10:11-21 (pp. 163-165). While this makes sense in terms of Jesus as the Good Shepherd, it would be difficult to evaluate how much a sheep can comprehend of a shepherd's leadership. It seems more probable to leave the connection of trust to the reality of vocal familiarity.

The shepherd's knowledge of and affection for the sheep establish a meaningful relationship between them. This relationship creates an environment where the sheep are able to discern and hear the voice of their shepherd. Consequently, they follow the shepherd as he leads them out of the sheep pen and into pasture. Underscoring the action of the sheep is the trust that they have placed in their shepherd. He is one who knows their name, calls them by that name, and faithfully leads them.

The disability-effective pastor is not only trustworthy, but also creates a community where trust is quickly visible and highly valued. The importance of this quality cannot be missed. Often times the disabled are the ones who are preyed upon by those who seek to do an individual harm through their own self-serving actions. A parent must get the sense that their child is safe when he or she is in the care of the pastor. Thus, the disability-effective church leader acts in ways that translates into the trust of both the parents and the disabled child. One way that this climate of trust can be established is through the pastor or church leader meeting with the parents of the disabled child. A discussion on individual strengths and enjoyments as well as parental cautions and concerns will begin to foster a level of trust between all parties. When this type of trust is achieved, the pastor communicates with their actions and attitudes that he or she is the defender of the defenseless and the voice for the voiceless.

Accessibility

The third relational quality is that of accessibility. In John 10:7-10, Jesus changes the metaphor so He is now the door or the gate to the sheep pen. In making this switch, Jesus is highlighting His dual role. He is the one who has sole access to the sheep, as well as the only way that the sheep can experience salvation and blessing.

These two functions are crucial to Ridderbos' understanding of John 10:7-10. Ridderbos (1997) understand Jesus's use of the door or gate to be indicative of His accessibility to the sheep. Only Jesus, as the gate, has the ability to get to the sheep. Thus, the shepherd serves to protect and keep his sheep safe. In this understanding, Ridderbos also acknowledges that Jesus is also the gate that leads to salvation for the sheep. In other words, the salvation, safety, and security of the sheep only happen if they go through the gate (p. 358). Hendriksen (1953) neatly summarizes a similar thought by pointing out that Jesus is both the door to the sheep and the door for the sheep. Thus, the dual nature of this illustration is appropriate because it highlights the in and out function of a door (p. 108).

However, consideration must be given to the fact that Jesus's extension or alteration of his metaphor rests on the fact that those listening to him did not understand it when it was first presented (John 10:6). Thus, it would be unwise to miss possible connections to the opening metaphor in John 10:1-6. These connections are something that Burge (2000) addresses in his understanding of John 10:7-10. Burge depicts the full image of this shepherd/gate metaphor when he points to both the security and the prosperity of the sheep. The picture being developed is one of vulnerable sheep that are protected from the predators that surround them. They cannot enter the sheep pen. However, the sheep are also well-fed since they are daily led to water and pastures. The sheep described in this metaphor are ones that are content and flourishing because of the skill of the shepherd (p. 290). Laniak (2006) agrees with Burge and supports this emphasis when both metaphors are understood together. Laniak writes of Jesus,

> He identifies himself as both door and shepherd. As the door, he is the exclusive means of entrance into the protected fold. As the shepherd, he is the one who leads the flock to pastures (abundant life). By both metaphors, Jesus contrasts himself with others—those who do not use the door and those who care for themselves rather than the flock. (p. 214)

Burge and Laniak are not the only commentators to recognize the benefits provided by Jesus in this continued metaphor. Much earlier, Westcott also made a similar connection to the robust nature of Jesus' two metaphors. However, Westcott sees three benefits provided by Jesus instead of just the two given by Burge. Westcott (1881/1978) sees in Jesus's pronouncement of "I am the door. If anyone enters by Me, he will be saved and will come in and go out and find pasture" (John 10:9), as Jesus's provision of the three elements in a full Christian life. These elements are safety, liberty, and support. Thus, Jesus as the gate is the one who can bring protection to His sheep. This sense of protection leads His sheep to living in a freedom that is represented by the in and out nature of their activities. Finally, it is because of Jesus that His sheep find the sustenance they need in their daily lives (p. 153).

What makes Jesus's door/gate pronouncement crucial for disability concerns is that this teaching follows the healing of a man born blind. In this healing Jesus, has just granted accessibility to a man who had never had any of it because of his disability. Malina and Rohrbaugh (1998) explain that in this time and culture the primary problem with sickness was the removing of the sick person from both their social mooring and social standing. Socialization between family members, friends, neighbors, and village mates was stopped. When healing occurred then restoration to the social network would be permitted (pp. 113-114).

Given this information, the once-blind man was shut out of any social network for his entire life. Additionally, he is known by his neighbors as a beggar (John 9:8). This way of life would have further devalued his social standing. The fact that John records the Pharisees having conversations with the neighbors and parents of the once-blind man is indicative of the fact that his life was not completely alone. However, these relationships could not have been deeply meaningful. Both the man's neighbors and his parents quickly recused themselves when pressed about the healing. Thus, Jesus's healing of the man provides him with accessibility to a social network within the followers of Jesus as well as eternal accessibility to Heaven.

This model of accessibility is an important consideration for the church as it thinks through purposeful disability ministry. Accessibility should be spiritual, physical, and, social. Spiritual accessibility takes into consideration a purposeful outreach to the disabled community so they have the opportunity to hear the gospel in a way that is understandable. It also studies what the process of discipleship should be like for those who, in their own way, have made a profession of faith in Jesus Christ. Spiritual accessibility also seeks to give those who have a disability the opportunity to use and share their spiritual gifts with the community of faith.

Physical accessibility means that a congregation has measured the ways that a disabled person might face challenges due to the church building as they participate in the full body—life of the church. Issues like handicapped parking or handicapped seating as well as access to restrooms are significant places to begin.

Social accessibility revolves around establishing a network that will support, encourage, and involve in the various programs of the church, those who are disabled. Additionally, it goes one step further and seeks to find ways to connect those who are disabled to other members of the church in ways that are not programmatically driven.

Only when each of these accessibility points are met will the church reverse the conclusion made by Nancy Eiesland (1994) when she wrote,

"For many disabled persons the church has been a 'city on a hill'—physically inaccessible and socially inhospitable" (p. 20).

Sacrifice

Jesus moves from describing the shepherd in John 10:1-15 to describing the good shepherd in John 10:11-18. In this progression, He identifies Himself as the Good Shepherd. The overuse of the word *good* in our culture can contribute to a misunderstanding of how the *good* in good shepherd should be defined. Laniak (2006) gives two reasons that *kalos*, the word used for *good*, should be translated as *model* instead of *good*. First, a common understanding of *good* often relates to nothing more than a moral quality. However, the term *kalos* implies more than this. "*Kalos* implies an attractive quality, something noble or ideal." Thus, a term like *model* better captures this imagery. Secondly, *kalos* implies emulation. As such, *model* also underscores this much more accurately than *good*. This emphasis on Jesus as the *model* shepherd also fits with John's perspective that Jesus is equipping the disciples to be like Him in both His life and death (p. 211).

Grammatically, it is best to understand that Jesus's movement from a shepherd to the Good Shepherd is about the type of shepherd one should use as a model. Yet, this is not simply a point of grammar. Jesus is stating that He alone is the Good Shepherd, and that those who follow Him should model His sense of shepherding. Jesus is not simply suggesting that one be a good shepherd by selecting a model that is comfortable for them. The designation of a good shepherd is not attributed to a subjective image. Instead, the Good Shepherd or Model Shepherd is Jesus Christ. One who is committed to Christ and follows His life acknowledges that they have a particular model in mind.

In order to demonstrate what makes up a model shepherd Jesus contrasts Himself to a hireling. Primarily He notes that the hireling does not care about the sheep and will run at the first sign of life-threatening trouble (John 10:12-13). The hired man places a greater value on his life than that of his sheep. Laniak (2006) recognizes that in making this contrast Jesus is pushing the boundaries of the metaphor. Shepherds would occasionally risk their life for their sheep. However, it would be unheard of for a shepherd to deliberately die for the protection and safety of the sheep he loves. Laniak perceptively summarizes, "Life for the predator entails death for the flock; life for the flock requires death for the shepherd" (p. 216).

In an escalating fashion, Keener (2003) describes the model shepherd as one who cared for his sheep even tending to sick sheep, so they were restored to health. The faithful and model shepherd's life was difficult and would require that he face predators in order to protect the sheep. Sometimes, facing a predator, robber, or thief may cost the faithful shepherd his life. However, a faithful shepherd who loves his sheep and would give up his own life for these sheep would astound listeners (pp. 813-814).

Both Laniak and Keener highlight the shock value of this further development in the teaching on the blind man's healing. Jesus, as the Model Shepherd, does something no shepherd in their right mind would consider doing. Yet, the Model Shepherd freely gives up His life for His own sheep. At the center of the Model Shepherd's self-sacrifice is a heart of love. The hired man runs when wolves, thieves, or robbers arrive. His self-preservation and commitment to the monetary gains of shepherding will not allow him to fight for the sheep, much less give his life for the sheep. The same cannot be said about the Model Shepherd.

Quasten (1948) highlights two reasons why the model shepherd will lay down his life for his sheep. First, the good shepherd cares for his sheep (John 10:11-13). Second, the good shepherd knows his sheep (John 10:14-15). These two reasons establish the primary character quality of the good shepherd. He is the one who is not afraid to give up his life for the sake of his sheep. Further, this self-sacrifice is indicative of the freedom of will possessed by the good shepherd (p. 161).

What does it look like for the model shepherd to care for his sheep? In other words, why would the model shepherd stay and die for his sheep rather than flee like a hired man does when trouble comes? Morris (1995) provides the answer as he explains the reasons for the actions of the hired man. He writes,

> The hired hand runs away not fortuitously, but because he is what he is, hired. His interest is in wages not sheep. He is not deeply concerned for the sheep. He is not involved in their situation. His

passions are not aroused. The interests of the sheep are not a lively concern for him. (p. 455)

The model shepherd on the other hand is concerned for his sheep. He is passionately involved in their situation so their existence is one of protection and provision (John 10:9). This is heightened by the fact that the model shepherd knows them. In fact, he calls them by name (John 10:3). Further, according to Jesus, that knowledge is similar to the way that He knows His Father God, and the way God the Father knows Him. Burge (2000) deftly explains what this means and the important application of the model shepherd's knowledge. He asserts,

> Perhaps the most startling feature of Jesus's interpretation is his description of the intimacy of the sheep and the shepherd. We have already learned that the sheep "know" the shepherd's voice (10:4), but now we learn that this knowledge is mutual and exhaustive (10:14). Moreover, the model for this intimacy is the mutual knowledge shared between the Son and the Father—and here Jesus slips out of the parable and speaks directly of himself and God (cf. Matt. 11:27). His profound relationship with God characterizes the intimacy he seeks with his followers (17:21); as he and the Father share profound love, so too Jesus and his flock share this quality of love. (p. 291)

Burge ties together both the caring or love of the model shepherd in John 10:11-13 and the knowledge of the good shepherd in John 10:14-15. In doing so, Burge (2000) is able to argue that the model for this mutual and exhaustive relationship is the reciprocal relational knowledge between Jesus and God (p. 291). Quasten (1948) also ties together this knowledge and love. He claims that the knowledge identified in John 10:14 is not a theoretical knowledge of "the Father's splendor, power, love, and fidelity." Rather, this knowledge represents "the most profound communion of love." This love is rooted in the attentive and considerate affection of the shepherd. This reciprocal knowledge underscored by love creates the readiness for the self-sacrifice of the shepherd (p. 162). The intimacy shared between God the Father and God the Son is the model for the intimacy of the shepherd and the sheep. It is a model that highlights a knowledge that goes beyond just knowing about someone. It's a loving knowledge of that person. Indeed, for the shepherd, it's a loving knowledge that will lead to his willingness to lay down his life for his sheep. This sacrifice is the ultimate blessing of eternal protection and provision.

What does sacrifice look like for the disability-effective pastor? It may look like the youth pastor who purposefully sets aside some of the latest visual effects used when leading worship because they may trigger a seizure in a youth group member diagnosed with epilepsy. Sacrifice may mean that, instead of one mission trip to a country where the lack of modern roads would be prohibitive for those in a wheelchair, two trips are planned so every member has the opportunity to participate in a mission trip. It is when sacrifice is most evident in church ministry that the relational qualities of the good shepherd are clearly being modelled.

Conclusion

While there may be a lack of literature on what constitutes a disability-effective pastor or church leader, it does not mean that a good guide is non-existent. A contextual examination of the good shepherd discourse clearly reveals four relational qualities that the disability-effective pastor possesses. The qualities of intimacy, trust, accessibility, and sacrifice demonstrate that he or she is a leader who sees disability ministry as something more than just a government issued blue sticker affixed to the front window of the church. Rather, the disability-effective pastor models the relational qualities of the good shepherd in such a way that he or she creates an inclusive atmosphere within the community of faith. It is an atmosphere that envisions the church as a hospital for the hurting rather than a country club for members only.

References

Beates, M. S. (2012). *Disability and the Gospel: How God uses our brokenness to display his grace.* Wheaton, Il: Crossway.

Block, J. W. (2002). *Copious hosting: A theology of access for people with disabilities.* New York, NY: The Continuum International Publishing Group Inc.

Brock, B. & Swinton, J. (Ed.). (2012). *Disability in the Christian tradition: A reader*. Grand Rapids, MI: Wm. B. Eerdmans Publishing Company.

Burge, G. M. (2000). John. In T. C. Muck (Ed.), *The NIV application commentary*. Grand Rapids, MI: Zondervan.

Carson, D. A. (Ed.). (1991). The gospel according to John. In *The pillar New Testament commentary*. Grand Rapids, MI: Wm. B. Eerdmans Publishing Company.

Comfort, P. W. & Hawley, W. C. (2007). *Opening John's gospel and epistles: Pastoral reflections on love, light, and logos*. Carol Stream, IL: Tyndale House Publishers.

Eiesland, N. L. (1994). *The disabled god: Towards a liberatory theology of disability*. Nashville, TN: Abingdon Press.

Eiesland, N. L. & Saliers, D. E. (Ed.). (1998). *Human disability and the service of God: Reassessing religious practice*. Nashville, TN: Abingdon Press.

Gangel, K. O. (2000). John. In M. Anders (Ed.), *Holman New Testament commentary*. Nashville, TN: Broadman and Holman Publishers.

Haenchen, E. (1984). John 2: A commentary on the gospel of John, Chapters 7-21. In

R. W. Funk (Ed.), *Hermeneia: A critical and historical commentary on the Bible*. Philadelphia, PA: Fortress Press.

Hendriksen, W. H. (1953). *The Baker New Testament commentary: Exposition of the gospel according to John*. (Vol. 1). Grand Rapids, MI: Baker Books.

Hubach, S.O. (2006). *Same lake, different boat: Coming alongside people touched by disability*. Phillipsburg, NJ: P&R Publishing Company.

Keener, C. S. (2003). *The gospel of John: A commentary*. (Vol. 1). Peabody, MA: Hendrickson Publishers.

Köstenberger, A. J. (2004). John. In R. Yarbrough and R. H. Stein (Ed.), *The Baker exegetical commentary on the New Testament*. Grand Rapids, MI: Baker Books.

Laniak, T. S. (2006). Shepherds after my own heart: Pastoral traditions and leadership. in the Bible. In D. A. Carson (Ed.), *New studies in biblical theology*. (Vol. 20). Downers Grove, IL: InterVarsity Press.

Malina, B. J. & Rohrbaugh, R. L. (1998). *Social-Science commentary on the gospel of John*. Minneapolis, MN: Fortress Press.

Morris, L. (1995). *The gospel according to John* (Rev. ed.). Grand Rapids, MI: Wm. B. Eerdmans Publishing Co.

Quasten, J. (1948). The parable of the good shepherd: Jn. 10:1-21. *The Catholic Biblical Quarterly, 10*(2), 151-169.

Rhodes, B. (2016). Signs and wonders: Disability in the fourth gospel. *The Journal of the Christian Institute on Disability. 5*(1), 53-75.

Ridderbos, H. N. (1997). *The gospel of John: A theological commentary*. Grand Rapids, MI: Wm. B. Eerdmans Publishing Co.

Sproul, R. C. (2009). *St. Andrew's expositional commentary: John*. Lake Mary, FL: Reformation Trust Publishing.

Tenney, M. C. (1964). Literary keys to the fourth gospel. *Bibliotheca Sacra 121*. 13-21.

Westcott, B. F. (1978). *The gospel according to St. John*. Grand Rapids, MI: Wm. B. Eerdmans Publishing Co. (Original work published 1881).

Wilson, C. T. (1906). *Peasant life in the Holy Land*. New York, NY: E. P. Dutton and Company.

Yong, A. (2011). *The Bible, disability, and the church: A new vision of the people of God*. Grand Rapids, MI: Wm. B. Eerdmans Publishing Co.

Author Biography

Dr. Chris Hulshof is an Associate Professor and Department Chair for Liberty University's School of Divinity. His teaching responsibilities include courses in Old Testament Survey, Inductive Bible Study, as well as a Theology of Suffering and Disability. Dr. Hulshof earned an Ed.D. from Southeastern Baptist Theological Seminary where his research was at the intersection of Disabilities, Theology, and Church Ministry. Catch Chris on twitter @US_EH.

Implicit Attitudes and Their affect on Autism in the Church

Dr. Brian Haack

Abstract: Given the rising prevalence of autism in the United States, this research explored data from 330 volunteer and paid children's ministry workers to determine their attitudes toward children with autism spectrum disorder (ASD), and the extent (if any) to which those attitudes might be correlated to the availability and sophistication (or lack thereof) of ASD accommodated ministry efforts. The sample group expressed significantly higher social distance preferences for children with ASD (indicating a statistically significant preference *not* to engage these children in ministry). Lastly, social distance attitudes were significantly correlated to the presence and sophistication of ASD accommodated ministry at the churches where the sample group members worshiped and served.

Introduction

As recently as the 1980's only one in every 2,000 children in the United States (US) was diagnosed with an autism spectrum disorder (ASD) (Doheny & Chang, n.d.). Over the last two decades, Autism diagnoses have risen sharply, with The Centers for Disease Control and Prevention (CDC) now estimating one of every 68 children in the US is diagnosed with ASD by their eighth birthday ("Autism 1 in 68," 2014). Accordingly, the National Institutes of Health (NIH) has made ASD one of its most important and highly funded neuropsychiatric research priorities (Fithri, 2011; "Estimates of NIH Funding," 2016).

Most biblically informed scholarly literature, which directly addresses ASD, has been produced recently. A great deal of that literature focuses on the low participation rates in faith communities from people with autism. Other authors have highlighted the virtually undisputed correlation between inclusive religious fellowships and an increase in perceived quality of life among those with ASD (Goldstein & Ault, 2015). In attempts to explain this apparent paradox (low participation despite increased quality of life) many authors seem inclined toward a presumption that low faith-group participation must be rooted in the observed lack of inclusion. This lack of inclusion in Christian fellowships is easily observed and not refuted here, but this study's data seems to contest the notion that lack of inclusion is *causal* to low participation (or vice versa). The data reviewed below suggests that tacit, stigmatizing attitudes within the church may be the factor that prevents development of the inclusion strategies we seek, while simultaneously contributing to the low participation rates observed.

REVIEW OF THE LITERATURE

Disability Theology

Outstanding theological commentary regarding the functional exclusion of the disabled from churches has been available for more than twenty years. Nancy Eiesland published *The Disabled God: Toward a Liberatory Theology of Disability* in 1994. In this groundbreaking work, Eiesland shares her experiences as a disabled believer whose church habitually disregarded her need for accommodation. This failure to accommodate passively prohibited her regular attendance and pushed her to the fringes of denominational fellowship. Her justifying theological discourse invites specific attention to Jesus' crucifixion wounds, which remained present in His resurrected body. Her example presents a thought provoking challenge to ideologies which presuppose how physical wholeness and even healing should be viewed (Eiesland, 1994). Fifteen years after Eiesland, Thomas Reynolds wrote *Vulnerable Communion: A Theology of Disability and Hospitality* (2008). This narrative described how the Reynolds family suffered a functional expulsion from their church fellowship due to their son's intellectual disabilities. Reynolds' accompanying theological commentary indicts the modern church for its beliefs, which seem to venerate the typically person to the exclusion of the disabled. The disabled, he says, tend to threaten our comfortable religious predilections toward concepts of wholeness and belonging (Reynolds, 2008). Amos Yong later published *The Bible, Disability, and the Church: A New Vision of the People of God* (2011). In it, he described the church's damaged understanding of the very humanity of disabled people. Yong (2011) says the church's views and responses to disability (particularly in the West) tend to grow from superficial readings of biblical texts, upon which we project western ideologies. These misplaced interpretations tend to relegate the disabled person to a place where they are marginalized, pitied, and objectified. Such placements predispose the church toward viewing the differently-abled person as an object lesson whose life serves no other purpose than the inspiration, admonition, or instruction of others. We fail to view the disabled person as fully human, intentionally created, loved by God, and endowed with attributes that contribute to the full beauty of the church (Yong, 2011).

Church Responses to Autism Spectrum Disorder

In addition to the discriminations noted by the authors above, contemporary popular literature also reveals extreme prejudices in the church's response to ASD. In one example, a Minnesota church told the Race family to keep their non-verbal autistic son at home due to his social and behavioral problems. The family refused, insisting their son needed and benefited from religious fellowship. The church responded by obtaining a criminal restraining order to keep their son away ("Church ban," 2008). Unfortunately, intolerance and prejudice go far beyond restraining orders. The Chicago Tribune reported in 2003 that an eight-year-old boy with autism in Milwaukee, Wisconsin was accidently killed at church when a pastor supposed he would exorcise evil spirits, which he [the pastor] believed were the cause of the boy's autistic behaviors. The force used to restrain the boy ended up suffocating him to death (McNeil & Biemer, 2003).

Sometimes, a church can indirectly harm children with autism by simply neglecting the challenges faced by families of those with ASD. Hartley et al. (2010) noted that families with a child on the autism spectrum suffer a significantly higher risk of divorce than families with no disabled children. Considering this risk, churches claiming to support marriage and the family should find ample cause for prioritizing a ministry for ASD. See figure 1 (next page).

Figure 1

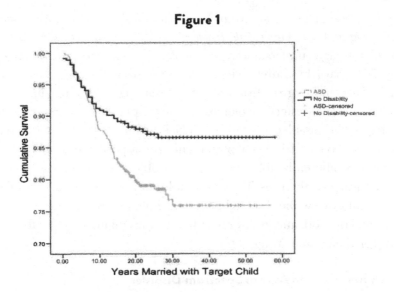

Figure 1 Autism's impact on marriage survivability from Hartley et al. (2010)

Figure 1 demonstrates that sampled couples with only non-disabled children (represented by the black lines) experienced a marriage failure rate of 13% over 20 years, which then stabilizes. By comparison, couples having at least one child with ASD (represented by the gray lines) experienced a significantly steeper rate of marriage failure, with 21% of marriages failing by year 20. The steep rate of marriage failure persists for another ten years, ultimately reaching 24% (nearly double the typical family rate of 13%) by the thirtieth year (Hartley et al., 2010).

The Role of Funding

Williams Webb (2012) identified a number of factors significantly correlated with ASD focused ministries. Exactly what an autism focused ministry *is* was not clearly defined, but churches with higher attendance, higher budgets, and higher numbers of paid staff were said to be significantly more likely to offer ASD related ministry services. The validity of correlation is not disputed here, but this should not lead us to a conclusion that ASD focused ministry is merely a product of financial solvency. Proclivities toward such conclusions quickly evaporate when one notes that most churches meeting the correlated factors do not offer ASD focused ministry efforts. With that in mind, one also cannot assume that the lack of ASD accommodated ministry is explained by financial limitations.

Social Perceptions of ASD

High functioning children with ASD may have extraordinary intellectual abilities while still experiencing severe problems with social integration, behavior, and communication (Chamberlain et al., 2013). These problems may cause them to avoid social situations, which further limits opportunities to practice and develop these skills (Hauck, Fein, Waterhouse, & Feinstein, 1995). Swaim & Morgan (2001) found that among all children with intellectual disabilities, those with high functioning ASD may be at highest risk for stigma and rejection due to attribution problems. Because high functioning ASD does not typically alter physical appearance, behavior problems associated with the disorder are often wrongly attributed to poor parenting or the child's assumed lack of discipline (Swaim & Morgan, 2001, p. 196). These attributions further interfere with social acceptance and the willingness of others to include and help the child with ASD develop socially.

When the child with ASD is more profoundly affected, changes in physical appearance may materialize to mitigate problems with attribution, but then, attribution problems are often replaced by assumptions that the child with profound ASD is intellectually inferior to others (Swaim & Morgan, 2001). Modern scholarship has done much to refute summary beliefs about intellectual inferiority in children with ASD, but these ideas persisted as the majority opinion about autism until well beyond the middle 1900's (Bonker & Breen, 2011; Grandin, 2006; Higashida, 2007; Moat, 2013). Despite recent enlightenment among scholars, obsolete attitudes may still persist among lay persons. Studies show that lowered expectations for the child with ASD will result in fewer opportunities for that child to participate, learn and socially benefit from instruction and the social learning opportunities available in these environments (Swaim & Morgan, 2001; Lumsden, 1997).

Social Distance Theory

Social distance research has shown that humans demonstrate consistently powerful attractions toward others who are perceived to be very much like self (Parrillo & Donoghue, 2013). This attraction is matched by an equally powerful tendency to exclude those perceived to be very different from self (Parrillo & Donoghue, 2013). When members of a divergent minority are consistently excluded from a highly-similar majority, the resulting exclusion creates a social distance phenomenon in which deprivation from social fellowship concurrently deprives the excluded class of the social, educational, and developmental benefits of belonging. Social distance liabilities can exacerbate exclusion-related problems over the lifespan. Such exacerbations can perpetuate (and widen) social distance gaps over time causing greater hardships for the disabled (Parrillo & Donoghue, 2013; Wilson & Scior, 2015).

Emory Bogardus (the father of Social Distance theory) found that where social contact, intimacy, and understanding increased, even vastly different groups could close social distance gaps and create mutually beneficial relationships (Wark & Galliher, 2007). Understanding and intimacy are contrasted in Social Distance Theory by prejudice. Bogardus defined prejudice as the "instinctive and spontaneous disposition to maintain social distances" (Wark & Galliher, 2007, p. 390). If intimacy leads to the closure of social distances; prejudice prevents such opportunities (Wark & Galliher, 2007). Bogardus' characterization of prejudice as a *spontaneous* and *instinctive* disposition strongly resembles words used today by modern attitude theorists to describe the formation of implicit attitudes in the *Value Account Model* (Betsch, Plessner, & Schallies, n.d.).

Attitude Theory

There is strong agreement among attitude theorists that attitudes find their formation and expression across affective, cognitive, and behavioral domains of human consciousness. Thus, any serious attitude-related research should explore and address all three domains if possible (Findler, Vilchinsky, & Werner, 2007). There may be some overlap between what Bogardus believed about the *instinctive* and *spontaneous* nature of social attractions and repulsions in the 1930s and what attitude theorist now affirm about the instinctive and spontaneous role of affective mental systems on attitude formation and subsequent behaviors. Implicit attitudes are thought to be most-responsible for negatively impacting the lives of the intellectually disabled regardless of the social group in question (Wilson & Scior, 2015).

Social Acceptability Bias

Attitude theorists and practitioners have long been concerned about the reliability of self-reported research instruments due to their potential sensitivity to Social Acceptability Bias (SAB). This sensitivity may compel investigational research participants to communicate opinions and attitudes, which do not represent their true beliefs. This is true even when the subject is guaranteed anonymity (Ouellette-Kuntz, Burge, Brown, & Arsenault, 2009). The misrepresentation of personal attitudes is not necessarily a deliberate attempt to deceive, but rather, a manifestation of the subject's perception that their opinions may be less socially acceptable than more socially acceptable beliefs of a perceived majority.

When subjects perceive their own beliefs are in conflict with the socially-accepted majority they may chose to express opinions that align with those majority norms rather than their own views. This reality makes investigating sensitive topics (like attitudes about disabled children) extremely difficult. Such difficulties are magnified when investigating church fellowships or other groups, which claim allegiance to doctrines that outwardly forbid such prejudices based on faith doctrines or policies (Swaim & Morgan, 2001; Wilson & Scior, 2015). The influence of SAB is exposed when self-reported attitudes conflict with observed or stated behaviors from the same subject. When these gaps appear, the researcher may assume study designs, research instruments, or both, have isolated *explicit* attitude statements (influenced by SAB) rather than those isolated from the *implicit* attitude constructs which tend to be less sensitive to SAB, and predict behavior (Betsch et al., n.d.; Swaim & Morgan, 2001; Wilson & Scior, 2015).

Explicit Versus Implicit Attitudes

Explicit attitudes are thought to be a product of cognitive ability, cumulative memory systems, and the brain's reflective processing capabilities (Betsch et al., n.d.). As one's consciousness of a socially acceptable (majority) belief system increases, the likelihood they will recite those beliefs as their own also increases (Betsch et al., n.d.; Wilson & Scior, 2015). Unlike *explicit* attitudes (which are very sensitive to SAB), *implicit* attitudes are "automatically activated" from the brain's affective processing systems (Wilson & Scior, 2015, p. 2). These affective expressions do not rely on cognitive abilities, memory, or reflective thought. Thus, if tested properly, even beliefs about very sensitive topics can be quickly recalled and expressed "without effort or intention" (Wilson & Scior, 2015, p. 2). With this in mind, we may summarize by saying implicit attitudes influence behavior intentions with little requirement for cognitive load or conscious thought. Because of how they are recalled and expressed, implicit attitudes are not dramatically affected or edited by sensitivities to SAB (Betsch et al., n.d.).

When researchers design test instruments and study methodologies to isolate implicit attitudes, research participants find the freedom they need to honestly express their true beliefs about even very sensitive topics. This is because the test instrument, method of administration (and perhaps other factors), allow the participant to bypass their own cognitive and reflective mental processes, which can edit expressions before they are articulated (Betsch et al., n.d.). Formatting limitations prohibit an exhaustive review of the specific controls used in this study for extracting implicit responses. Nevertheless, the author must report here that the research design, test instruments, and methods of administration were carefully engineered to optimize the probability of extracting responses from the sample group's affective mental processes and implicit attitudinal constructs.

The Research

Method

The research sample was restricted to Southern Baptists children's ministry workers in the state of North Carolina. Each of the 330 research participants in the sample completed an anonymous on-line survey in which they answered test items from multiple instruments, presented randomly and concurrently in what appeared (to them) to be a single survey.

All controls in this study were carefully constructed to elicit and isolate responses from the subject's affective mental constructs in accordance with recommendations from the *Value Account Model* (Betsch et al., n.d.). The specific intent of these controls was to commandeer the respondent's cognitive, memory, and reflective mental capabilities and to deflect them toward superfluous details. The rationale for doing so is to bind up these capabilities making them unavailable to edit the subject's responses to value charged information in the test items.

Tests Used

Autism Ministry Activities & Attitudes Questionnaire (AMAAQ)

With advice from numerous published and personally acquainted scholarly colleagues, this researcher developed, validated, and deployed the Autism Ministry Activities and Attitudes Questionnaire (AMAAQ). This test is a specially designed social distance research instrument intended for use in Christian ministry settings. The goal of AMAAQ is to extract, quantify, and compare the test subject's social distance attitudes toward typically developing children and children with ASD. In accordance with recommendations from Findler et al. (2007), the AMAAQ tests affective, cognitive, and behavioral attitudinal domains. Considering Findler and colleagues' painstaking work in the development and validation of test items in their *Multiple Attitudes Scale* (MAS), this researcher mimicked the language and construct used in the MAS wherever possible. The significant contributing influence of Findler et al. (2007), was augmented by the use of video vignettes and a two-phased, indirect-examination (IE) procedure similar (though not identical) to that used by Swaim & Morgan (2001). Other theoretical contributors to the AMAAQ's construction and methods of administration included Betsch et al. (n.d.), Wilson & Scior (2015) and Yuker, Block, & Younng (1970).

Procedure

The testing protocol required each research participant to take the AMAAQ twice. The two-test method follows a pre-test, treatment, post-test format. The first iteration (AMAAQ-1) asks participants to read a brief fictional narrative and view a 50-second video vignette. The narrative explains the unexpected addition of two typically developing children to a children's ministry class. The video portrays the children joining the hypothetical class. Using IE techniques, participants are asked to consider only the information in the narrative and video to derive and report a level of agreement or disagreement with 15 rapid-fire, Likert-type test items. The score of AMAAQ-1 becomes the respondent's baseline score.

With no break, the subject proceeds immediately to the second iteration (AMAAQ-2). This test (like the first) is preceded by a brief narrative and 50-second video (*the treatment*). The second narrative (like the first) discloses the unexpected addition of two children to a children's ministry class. They are the same age, race, and sex as those described in the first, but these children are described as having some impairment to their communication, behavior, and social abilities, which are readily apparent when the subject views the 50-second video portraying the two children. After the treatment, research participants are once again asked to indicate their level of agreement or disagreement to an identical list of 15 rapid-fire, Likert-type test items. The score of AMAAQ-2 becomes the comparative post-test score.

AMAAQ Results

With a range of zero (0) to 60 on both tests, the results of AMAAQ-1 (baseline) produced a test population $\bar{x} = 38.97$, a median $= 41$, and a mode $= 45$. The AMAAQ-2 (post-treatment) score distributions produced a $\bar{x} = 33.33$, a median $= 33$, and mode $= 29$. The baseline and post-test results were compared using a paired samples *t-test*. Results indicated a statistically significant preference for greater social distances between the sample group and children with ASD than for typically developing children. This indicates a statistically significant attitudinal unwillingness to engage children with ASD in ministry *(p = < .001)*. According to Gliem & Gliem (2003) both AMAAQ tests demonstrated *excellent* internal consistency and reliability via Cronbach's alpha (α) tests ($\alpha = > .900$).

Sophistication of Autism Ministry Survey (SAMS)

One weakness in other autism related ministry literature is that *autism ministry* is loosely (if at all) defined. The SAMS proposes a structure for correcting this trend and provides a grading rubric, which measures ASD directed ministry efforts against tangible, objective standards along five functional domains. They are:

1) Welcome and integration plans for children with ASD
2) Training on ASD for Children's ministry workers/volunteers
3) Availability of ASD specialists/experts for consultation
4) ASD-motivated classroom and teaching modifications
5) Methods to help children with ASD serve, share faith, and evangelize others.

Each question on the SAMS represents one of the five domains above and asks participants to select the response that best-represents their *personal experience or knowledge* of accommodations made under each domain at their church. Selectable choices under each question represent a continuum (or a *spectrum*, if you will), which begins with *no accommodation* (scored with zero points) to responses that represent a *mature and sustained accommodation* (scored with five points). Scored answers create a possible composite scoring range of zero (0) to 25. For example, a research participant who reports a mature and sustained accommodation across all five domains would have a composite SAMS score of 25. One reporting no accommodation at all across all five domains would have a composite score of zero (0). The 330-member sample group recorded SAMS composite scores ranging from one (1) to 22. The sample's score distributions and performance rubric (by number and percentage of respondents) is reported in Table 1 on the next page.

Table 1 SAMS Results – North Carolina's ASD Accommodated Ministry

Composite SAMS Score	Respondent's Characterization of ASD accommodated ministry at their church	$N = X$ $\% = X$
0-5	No genuine ministry is being attempted for children with ASD. No active plans to welcome children with ASD in the future.	$N = 43$ $\% = 13$
6-10	Children with ASD are *theoretically welcome* but are not meaningfully accommodated to help them participate in congregational ministry and worship.	$N = 160$ $\% = 48.5$
11-15	Children with ASD are being practically welcome and accommodated in a genuine (but limited) ministry effort.	$N = 98$ $\% = 30$
16-20	Children with ASD are receiving intentional, accommodated, and sustained ministry but are not developing their gifts or being groomed for service to the church or for evangelism of others.	$N = 25$ $\% - 7.5$
20-25	Children with ASD are meaningfully accommodated, groomed to serve according to their abilities and gifts, and are being taught how to help others come to faith in Christ as fully participating members of The Body.	$N = 4$ $\% - 1$
		$N = 330$ $N = 100$

SAMS Results

As noted above, SAMS Scores were grouped in five point increments which quantified performance across the five functional domains. The distribution of composited SAMS scores from the 330-member sample yielded a $\bar{x} = 9.49$, a median $= 9$, and an overwhelming modal score $= 6$. A large percentage of the sample (48.5%) initially reported that their church *welcomes children with ASD*, but from a functional standpoint, these same respondents disclosed that their churches do not offer any specific efforts to help the autistic child overcome challenges to genuinely participate in worship and ministry. Accordingly, subjective claims to *welcome* those with ASD dissolve under practical scrutiny.

Another 13% of the sample indicated their church makes absolutely no claim whatsoever to welcome children with ASD, nor do they have plans to develop such capabilities in the future. This means that functionally speaking, 61.5% of the churches represented by the sample group affirmed they have no meaningful response to autism, despite the growing body of autism-relevant literature and autism's rapidly growing presence in society. The scores on SAMS were significantly correlated with scores on the AMAAQ test. The agreement between SAMS and AMAAQ seems to offer criterion validity to both tests, affirming their accuracy and cross validating their results while successfully capturing the attitudinal realities of the status quo.

Implications for Ministry Leaders

Given the firsthand accounts of disability exclusion offered by scholars like Eiesland (1994), Reynolds (2008), and Yong (2011), along with the data from the present research, we can no longer deny that exclusion of the disabled from the church is a problem. This research seems to conclusively affirm that people with ASD are indeed experiencing a specific brand of social exclusion from Southern Baptist churches. Without intentional effort to oppose this trend, the church is likely to maintain what has (thus far) proven to be a comfortable status quo in which children with ASD are instinctively and spontaneously excluded from the typical majority.

Practical Applications

1. Identify social distance realities in your church.

Eiesland (1994) rightly noted that insisting the disabled are *welcomed* does not make it so. The fact that social exclusion occurs in human societies is enough evidence to presume it occurs in the church. Genuine *welcoming* cannot be established by policy or doctrine, but only by those who will serve the target population. A properly administered and interpreted

AMAAQ analysis can give you a proven, data-supported picture of your church's social distance realities toward ASD.

2. Evaluate ASD ministry efforts against standard criteria.

Despite actively asserting their churches *welcomed* children with ASD, 61.5% of the 330-member sample could not identify anything their church did to help autistic children participate in corporate fellowship. When claims were examined against actual performance criteria only four (1%) of the 330 churches represented were found to have a mature and sustained ASD focused ministry. Pastors are urged to appraise their own church's ministry efforts for children with ASD against actual performance standards like those established in the SAMS.

3. Adapt and Conquer

This research model has proven to be theoretically-sound and field-proven. Accordingly, it can be easily adapted to study how social distance realities may be impacting your other ministry efforts. Assuming tests are properly administered, data properly collected, analyzed and interpreted, this model could be used to study the impact of social distance phenomena on ministry efforts aimed at the homeless, addicts, prison inmates, sex-workers, or any other socially marginalized group.

Conclusion

Until now, the low attendance rates among people with ASD in Christian fellowships were presumed to be related to a simple lack of knowledge or an operational inability to implement autism-specific accommodations. This study, however, exposes stigmatizing attitudes among 330 Southern Baptist church members who strongly preferred not to engage children on the autism spectrum in ministry. Moreover, the sample members' individual attitudes were significantly correlated with the presence and maturity of ASD focused ministry at their places of worship.

The data clearly indicates that children with ASD are functionally excluded from Southern Baptist Church life as a matter of attitudinal preference; not because of ignorance or operational deficits (as previously believed). The data also confirms that these realities are not isolated aberrations but are widespread and normative. Unchallenged, these normative attitudinal realities settle into passive cultures, which are unwilling (and thus, unable) to invite and welcome the regular, consistent attendance of families with children on the spectrum.

References

Betsch, T., & Plessner, H. (n.d.). The value-account model of attitude formation. Retrieved from https://www.researchgate.net/publication/265744379_1_The_value-account_model_of_attitude_formation.

Bonker, E. M., & Breen, V. G. (2011). *I am in here*. Grand Rapids, MI: Revell.

CDC estimates 1 in 68 children has been identified with autism spectrum disorder. (2014). Retrieved from http://www.cdc.gov/media/releases/2014/p0327-autism-spectrum-disorder.html.

Chamberlain, P. D., Rodgers, J., Crowley, M. J., White, S. E., Freeston, M. H., & South, M. (2013, September 4). A potentiated startle study of uncertainty and contextual anxiety in adolescents diagnosed with autism spectrum disorder. *Molecular Autism*. http://dx.doi.org/10.1186/2040-2392-4-31.

Doheny, K., & Chang, L. (n.d.). Autism cases on the rise; reason for increase a mystery. Retrieved from http://www.webmd.com/brain/autism/searching-for-answers/autism-rise.

Eiesland, N. E. (1994). *The disabled God: Toward a liberatory theology of disability*. Nashville, TN: Abingdon Press.

Estimates of funding for various research, condition, and disease categories (RCDC). (2016). Retrieved from https://report.nih.gov/categorical_spending.aspx.

Findler, L., Vilchinsky, N., & Werner, S. (2007). The multidimensional attitudes scale toward persons with disabilities (MAS): Construction and validation. *Rehabilitation Counseling Bulletin, 50*, 166-176. Retrieved from http://eds.a.ebscohost.com.

Fithri, H. (2011). Religious therapy as one of an alternative ways in getting educational betterment for children with autism spectrum disorder. *Procedia—Social and Behavioral Sciences, 29*, 1782-1787. Retrieved from https://doi.org/10.1016/j.sbspro.2011.11.425.

Gliem, J. A., & Gliem, R. R. (2003). *Calculating, interpreting and reporting Cronbach's Alpha reliability coefficient for Likert-type scales.* Paper presented at the Midwest Research to Practice Conference in Adult, Continuing and Community Education, Columbus, OH. Retrieved from http://www.ssnpstudents.com/wp/wpcontent/uploads/205/02/Gliem-Gliem.pdf.

Goldstein, P., & Ault, M. J. (2015). Including individuals with disabilities in a faith community: A framework and example. *Journal of Disability & Religion, 19*(1), 1-14. http://dx.doi.org/ 10.1080/23312521.2015.992601.

Grandin, T. (2006). *Thinking in pictures, expanded edition: My life with autism* (Exp ed.). New York, NY: Vintage Books.

Hammett, J. (2007). The Doctrine of Man. In D. L. Akin (Ed.), *A theology for the church* (pp. 340-409). Nashville, TN: B&H.

Hartley, S. L., Barker, E. T., Seltzer, M. M., Floyd, F., Greenburg, J., Orsmond, G., & Bolt, D. (2010). Relative Risk and Timing of Divorce in Families With Children With an Autism Spectrum Disorder. *J fam Psychol, 24*(4), 449-457. http://dx.doi.org/10.1037/a0019847.

Hauck, M., Fein, D., Waterhouse, L., & Feinstein, C. (1995, December). Social initiations by autistic children to adults and other children. *Journal of Autism and Developmental Disorders, 25*(6), 579-595. Retrieved from http://ehis.ebscohost.com/ehost/.

Higashida, N. (2007). *The reason I jump.* New York, NY: Random House.

Hoekema, A. A. (1986). *Created in the image of God.* Grand Rapids, MI: William B Eerdmans.

Howard, T. A. (2013). The promise of the image. In *Imago Dei Human dignity in ecumenical perspective* (pp. 15-38). Washington, DC: Catholic University of America Press.

McNeil, B., & Biemer, J. (2003, August 25). Autistic boy, 8, dies in Milwaukee church. *Chicago Tribune.* Retrieved from articles/chicagotribune.com/2003-08-25/.

Moat, D. (2013). *Integrative psychotherapeutic approaches to Autism Spectrum Conditions: Working with hearts of glass*. London, UK: Jessica Kingsley.

Mom fights church ban on her autistic son. (2008). Retrieved from http://www.nbcnews.com/id/24920240/#.Um8mh_mbMRI.

Ouellette-Kuntz, H., Burge, P., Brown, H., & Arsenault, E. (2009, April 12). Public attitudes towards individuals with intellectual disabilities as measured by the concept of social distance. *Journal of Applied Research in Intellectual Disabilities*, *23*, 132-142. http://dx.doi.org/10.1111/j.1468.2009.00514.x.

Parrillo, V. N., & Donoghue, C. (2013). National social distance study: Ten years later. *Sociological forum*, *28*, 597-614. http://dx.doi.org/10.1111/socf.12039.

Reynolds, T. E. (2008). *Vulnerable communion A theology of disability and hospitality*. Grand Rapids, MI: Brazos Press.

Swaim, K. F., & Morgan, S. B. (2001). Children's attitudes and behavioral intentions toward a peer with autistic behaviors: Does a brief educational intervention have an effect? *Journal of Autism and Developmental Disorders*, *31*, 195-205. Retrieved from http://eds.b.ebscohost.com.ezproxy.sebts.edu/.

Wark, C., & Galliher, J. F. (2007). Emory Bogardus and the origins of Social Distance Scale. *The American Sociologist*, *38*, 383-395. http://dx.doi.org/10.1007/s12108-007-9023-9.

Williams Webb, M. (2012). *A study of churches as a source of support for families with children on the autism spectrum* (Doctoral dissertation, University of Tennessee at Chattanooga). Retrieved from http://scholar.utc.edu/cgi/viewcontent.cgi?article=1087&context=theses.

Wilson, M. C., & Scior, K. (2015). Implicit attitudes towards people with intellectual disabilities: Their relationship with explicit attitudes, social distance, emotions and contact. *PLoS ONE*, *10*. http://dx.doi.org/10.1371/journal.pone.0137902.

Yong, A. (2011). *The Bible, disability and the church: A new vision of the people of God*. Grand Rapids, MI: William B. Eerdman's.

Yuker, H. E., Block, J. R., & Younng, J. H. (1970). *The measurement of attitudes toward disabled persons*. Retrieved from National Institutes of Health Website: http://www.ncbi.nlm.nih.gov/.

Author Biography

Dr. Haack currently serves as an adjunct professor in the Moore Graduate School of Education at Piedmont International University in Winston Salem, North Carolina. He is currently developing a book manuscript for publication while seeking a full-time academic appointment.

Autism and The Church: A Case Study of the Experiences of Four Children with Autism in Evangelical Churches

Dr. Yvana Uranga-Hernandez

Abstract: Autism affects 1 in 68 children according to the Center for Disease Control (CDC, 2016). Research suggests that church attendance and believing in God helps parents cope with children with autism and improve quality of life (Lee, Harrington, Louie, and Newschaffer, 2008). This qualitative research is a case study of four children with autism that seeks to understand their experiences in church settings. The data includes 23 observations and 11 interviews. Several themes and subthemes emerged to answer the research questions regarding the advantages and disadvantages of both fully included and self contained classrooms in children's ministry. To conclude, the study offers several implications and recommendations to different groups in the church: pastors, church volunteers, parents, and the overall church body.

Introduction

Autism affects 1 in 68 children according to the Center for Disease Control (CDC, 2016). With such a large amount of the population being affected with autism, it is of utmost importance the church makes an effort to provide a place for families dealing with autism. According to Lewis (2009), there is considerable research that links health and disabilities to spirituality and faith. She states, "it would be reasonable to hypothesize that children with autistic spectrum conditions (and other disabilities) also gain similar support from such beliefs" (p. 66). From an individualistic perspective, the importance of this study can be strictly about children with autism and their spiritual well-being however, since no one person lives independent of others, it is important to consider the needs of the family. This article will argue that the church can be a resource for families that are struggling with raising a child with autism, it can attempt to better equip these families, and show their support by providing programs to help the child and the family. In Matthew 22:37-40 Jesus replied:

> 'Love the Lord your God with all your heart and with all your soul and with all your mind.' This is the first and greatest commandment. And the second is like it: 'Love your neighbor as yourself.' All the Law and the Prophets hang on these two commandments. (NIV)

Therefore, the church body must meet the needs of children with autism and their families, if not we fail to obey and live out the two greatest commandments given to us. The following paragraphs will provide specific details as to what research says families with children with autism go through in their daily lives and offer a focus on how the church can provide support.

Research reports that mothers with children with disabilities often suffer from depression and mental illness at a much higher degree than those with typically developing (reaching expected developmental milestones) children (Bailey et al, 2007; Zablotsky, Anderson, & Law, 2013). Research also suggests that depression levels and hopelessness levels of mothers increase, and greater hopelessness levels indicate higher levels of depression (Ceylan & Aral, 2007).

In another article the emotional well-being of the married couple was taken into account. Married couples who have a child with autism have more parental stress, lower social support, and relationship satisfaction than couples who do not have a child with autism (Brobst, Clopton, & Hendrick, 2009). Hartley, Barker, Seltzer, Greeberg, Bolt, Floyd, and Orsmond (2010) found higher rates of divorce in parents who have children with autism than those who do not as well as a "longer period of vulnerability for divorce" (p. 455).

The importance of children with autism attending church, becomes two fold: first, the spiritual formation of the child is a concern and second, the need for support of the family, specifically the parents. Newsome's (2000) research further established parents of children with autism have needs that are highly influenced by their child. Current research indicates parents need support in their everyday lives to cope with how to raise their children; however, research suggests that this support is often the missing component in many families raising children with autism (Ramisch et al., 2013).

Since the church is a place offering support in both raising children and in strengthening marriages, congregations should provide support to this specific population. To further strengthen the case for the need of church involvement in the lives of these families, especially young families with children with autism, we can look at a study by Gray (2006). Over a ten-year period, he studied families with children with autism and found that coping strategies and the problems of parenting a child with autism changed over time. One of the findings of this study was parents were now relying on God as a way of explaining their child's situation.

If we take this information along with the study from Lee, Harrington, Louie, and Newschaffer (2008), we see church attendance and a belief in God as a positive factor for the life of families. This finding agrees with the Lee et al. (2008) study that church could improve quality of life for these families; therefore, involvement with a faith community can become a way for families who have children with autism to cope with life. The idea is then to fully include children with autism into faith communities, similar to how the public school system mainstreams students within the autism spectrum into the regular education classroom.

Full inclusion is the philosophy that all children should be educated together in an effort to maximize their learning and gain the most benefit possible from participating with typically developing children (Thousand & Villa, 1999; Bennett, Deluca, & Bruhns, 1997). Full inclusion is widely debated in the public-school system and commonly implemented, but should it be the same in the church? Is full inclusion the only way to serve children with autism or will a special needs ministry with a dedicated class for children with disabilities best meet their needs? By understanding their experiences and not just focusing on what others state, we may be able to improve on how we meet the needs of children with autism, and by meeting their needs we can also serve their families.

Research Purpose

According to Carlson (2016), "there is a great need for churches to better plan for the inclusion of individuals with special needs…" (p.1). There is also need for further research on children with disabilities in the church. Most research has "focused on children with disabilities within the domain of public school education" (p. 1). This study explored the experiences of four male children with autism and their participation in church. The boys were given pseudonyms used throughout this article: Matthew, Kevin, Oscar, and Sam.

Oscar and Sam attend a church that practices full inclusion, and Matthew and Kevin attend a church with a special needs class. The purpose of this qualitative case study was to explore the experiences of the children in order to better address their needs and provide recommendations to churches regarding ministry to children with autism.

Methods

In an effort to establish construct validity during this study "multiple sources of evidence" were utilized as part of the study (Yin, 2014, p. 47). All required documents were completed, submitted, and approved by the Protection of Human Rights and Research Committee (PHRCC) at Biola University. Data for this research project was collected between the summer of 2015 and winter of 2016. Data included 23 observations and 11 interviews. The sample was a purposeful sample: four boys, ages of five to eleven, diagnosed with autism, attending four different churches within 30 miles of L.A. County. Each child and their family attended their church for at least three months. Those interviewed were the classroom teacher and her/his helpers as well as the Children's Ministry Director/Pastor or Disability Ministry Director. One parent of each child was also interviewed. The interviews corroborated what was observed of the child's behavior at church

The recruitment process was to identify nearby churches that host children's ministry programs as part of their weekly worship services. The children's ministry program needed to have some mention of how they met the needs of children with special needs. Two of the programs selected have self-contained classrooms for children with disabilities and the other two fully integrate children in to their children's ministry program. Personal contacts were used as part of the recruitment process. Relationships with the Children's Ministry Director/Pastor or the Disability Ministry Director were established and through these introductions were made to families willing to participate. Written informed consent was received from all of the adult participants and was given for the participation of the minors in this study.

Results

Themes and subthemes arose from the data to answer the research questions regarding the advantages and disadvantages of fully included programs and self-contained classrooms in a church setting. This article will focus on the following themes Church Resources, Classroom Participation, and Barriers to Successfully Including Children in the Church.

Church Resources

One of the first themes in this study was the difference in church resources. The issue of curriculum, staff to do the work, teacher experience, and program availability were observed during observations and heard in interviews. These subthemes are discussed below.

Curriculum. The curriculum was significantly different across settings. There was no curriculum used with Sam during his time in the nursery. At Oscar's church, a story was read from a children's Bible; however, the craft was unrelated to the story. Matthew's classroom did use a curriculum with a Bible story and related craft; however, the classroom teacher shared the following:

> We've talked a lot about the desire to have a curriculum that's more closely aligned with what they're using in the regular Sunday school setting. I would like a curriculum that engages the students more. My ideal curriculum is biblically based, sometimes I read

the story and then the Bible verse at the end and I'm like how does
this even go? It feels like it waters down the gospel so much they
don't really get the essence of what it is to be a believer. They don't
make connections, so telling a separate story about Joseph and
how he lost his coat and how we need to be nice to our neighbors,
and it's like, oh gosh, but that's not really the essence of the story.
Yeah, we should be kind to our family, but there's more to it. They
have a lot of capability to understand, it just has to be presented
in different ways. We have that ability we just need the resources.

The curriculum used in Kevin's class was significantly different. The
storytellers used soft voices and were intentional on how they spoke and
what they asked. They used specific manipulatives for each story. When
asked about the curriculum the Director of Disability stated, "This curriculum is Montessori based, so it is great for our kids."

Teacher Experience. In all four settings, the teacher experience
was different in the amount of time they had working with children with
disabilities, as well as whether or not they had experience working with
children with disabilities. In Matthew's and Kevin's classrooms, both lead
teachers had experience working with children with special needs. Oscar's
teacher had worked with children with disabilities for nine months and
Sam's teacher had worked in the nursery for a total of four years, including
one year working with children with autism.

Number of Staff. The number of staff available also differed. Matthew's and Kevin's classes were heavily staffed. They had a ratio of one
helper to a child and two adults to a child. During one observation, Oscar's
class had nine children to two adults and Sam's class had three adults to
6-7 kids. The Disability Director in Matthew's church also referenced the
number of staff volunteers available for her stating one of the reasons the
curriculum was not changed because she was the only paid staff and she
was unable to devote time to it.

Program Availability. Not all churches have a class available for
children with disabilities. Those that do not can still welcome children and
their families. Sam's church did not have a specific class for children with
disabilities; however, the Assistant Children's Ministry Director expressed

her willingness to provide what Sam needed to function in a preschool class.

> On Wednesday nights we have a program during the school year with about 20 children in the classroom—but there are about four people...three adults and one teenager with the preschoolers and kindergarteners...We could put another person in there just to walk around with Sam.

Program availability was also discussed by all four parents.

Children's Participation The second theme was children's participation. This theme had two main subthemes: parental choice and child's level of engagement.

Parental Choice. Regardless of whether the church had a separate program for children with disabilities or whether they fully included the child, it was evident that the specific program the child participated in was due to parental choice in all four cases.

Child's Level of Engagement. Each child's level of engagement was unique to who they were and to their participation in their classroom. Some of them were able to engage and interact with less assistance, but overall all four of them required some type of assistance. Their level of engagement indicated that given specific activities, the children did attend to what was happening in the classroom. Although Sam was in the nursery and there was no set routine or program available for him, he did demonstrate the ability to engage with the adults around him.

Oscar was engaged on most observations with some of the storytelling; however, he required a prompt to sit down, or being held by an adult. Matthew was the most engaged; however, Matthew had one-on-one assistance. There were times when he had two peers working on keeping him engaged. Matthew participated in story time, singing, and various activities.

Kevin also required assistance to remain engaged. During the first observation the teacher told the story of Baby Jesus and Kevin laid on the floor. He grabbed the figurines the teacher was using, but was quickly asked not to. He stopped touching the figurines, but continued laying on the floor. The Lead teacher tried to get him up, but he just laid there. Before the story ended Kevin got up and ran to the other side of the room.

The lead teacher brought him back and he laid on the floor again; however, this time on a beanbag. He continued listening to the story.

Barriers to Successfully Including Children in the Church

Research addresses different barriers for why full inclusion does not always work. One barrier is negative attitudes of people around the children (Bennett, Deluca, & Bruhns, 1997).

Attitudes. Attitudes of adults toward some of the children were observed in the words used and body language expressed. In other instances, the attitude was apparent when the adult said or did nothing at all. On the first evening at Sam's church it was unclear what class Sam would be included for participation. What was evident, was the nursery workers did not want him in their class. The nursery workers told Sam's dad, Sam could not be in there and sent him to the preschool room. In the preschool class a young man said to Dad, "I have worked with him before," when Dad said "Let me explain about my son." The young man looked at the boy and said, "He will be fine in here." A few minutes later the classroom teacher arrived and asked why Sam was not in the nursery where he would be able to play. She told Dad the preschool class would be doing story time and there were scissors and markers involved; therefore, Sam would be safer in the nursery. During the second evening another child that looked very much like Sam was taken to the preschool class. The teacher insisted this child not come in her class but go to the nursery. The child's dad explained the child belonged in her class. When she realized he was not Sam, she allowed him in.

Matthew's teacher also spoke about attitudes as barriers, but she shared about those barriers being the reason parents attended her church. "And I've heard several times, sadly, from parents, that they had to leave the church they were going to because the church kicked them out." Previously, she had made a comment pointing to barriers within her own church. "I don't see the church going out of the way to accommodate parents for women's events or their families for family nights. They don't really include them in their thoughts of what might be needed for families to participate."

Although no specific comments were made about Oscar, attitudes were observed in some of the helpers. Through observation and in their inattentiveness, it appeared some of the helpers fostered a negative attitude toward Oscar; however, it is impossible to say if this was simply due to not understanding how to work with him.

Lack of Resources. As previously stated, the difference in resources was evident between churches. Lack of resources is a huge barrier when attempting to meet the needs of children with autism and their families. The lack of resources was training in the area of disability, curriculum, and volunteers.

Discussion

This qualitative case study sought to explore the experiences of children with autism in church. The experience of church attendance and participation for children with autism was as unique as the child himself. Each of them participated at a level allowed by who they are, as well as by their environment. The interactions of the adults and peers also influenced their participation and experiences.

According to the adults surrounding the child, the advantages of having a child participate in a fully included program were as follows: the child was with children he could learn from, the child was in the class the parents requested, and he was in a safe environment. While these advantages appeared to be true for Oscar, they weren't for Sam. Sam was left alone with little interaction. Being in a fully included program was a disadvantage due to the severity of his autism and the lack of knowledge, training, and preparedness at his church. People simply were unsure how to interact with him. For Sam, attending a fully included nursery with no curriculum, was even more of a disadvantage. At no time was any story of Jesus shared in class.

Another disadvantage for both boys dealt with the lack of staff available for each of their classes and the lack of program availability. Most of the barriers were seen in both situations as well, including lack of resources and negative attitudes. The first negative attitude in Sam's case was the clear rejection of the nursery workers. They simply did not want Sam in the nursery room. The reason given by the workers was his age; however, it is possible that they did not know what to do with him due to his disability. The attitude against having him in class was also observed in the preschool teacher, even though she, has experience with children with disabilities, according to the assistant pastor. The second negative attitude observed in Sam's case was the worker ignoring Sam. Some of the people at church simply acted like he was not there.

One advantage for both Matthew and Kevin in participating in a separate environment was being served by people who knew exactly how to work with each of them. Another advantage was the program fit as it allowed the boys to attend church with their families.

It appears a combined model would maximize the advantages and minimize the disadvantages for Sam by providing an environment that would be conducive to his type of learning and interaction. An area of focus would be providing people who were trained to assist him. Sam could be in a program that would meet his individual needs and yet allow him to see typical children's behavior. It is definitely possible for Sam's experience to improve; however, the church first needs to develop a plan for how to assist children with disabilities.

In Oscar's case, there were also ways to minimize the disadvantages and maximize the advantages. A class geared towards children with disabilities or at least some small group time just for students with disabilities would help. Increasing church resources would also change things for the better; specifically, training for the teacher and staff and appropriate curriculum.

While Matthew's class also needed an improved curriculum, Kevin's program appeared to be doing quite well with only one observation when there was not enough staff to assist in the classroom. The themes from this study answered the research questions; however, in answering these questions another question comes to mind.

What exactly is the goal for children with disabilities attending church? If it is to teach them the love of Jesus and allow them to be exactly whom Jesus has designed them, then it should be in an environment that is accepting and conducive to their learning style. For each child, the issue of whether full inclusion or a separate classroom environment is most appropriate is an individual question. The ideal situation would be each child participating in a program that best fits their needs; however, because churches have different types of programs the ideal environment is not always possible. Given that there are several factors to put in place at every church when a child with autism and their family show up, the church must be equipped and ready to welcome them with open arms and fully assure them there is a place for them.

Implications for Church Ministry

There are several implications that arise from this research and to make these implications easier to understand, they are categorized in response to who needs to know about them.

Pastors

As leaders of the church, understanding disabilities is essential to having the congregation understand the importance of this issue. A course in seminary on child development or Christian education that includes information on autism and other disabilities would be helpful. For churches that actually have a children's ministry director or a disability ministry director, this may be easier to accomplish. If a pastor is unable to take on this part of the congregation due to his other responsibilities, then having someone on staff to be the point of contact is critical. Without that person, when a family approaches a church and nobody knows how to serve them, the family may feel ostracized.

Church Volunteers

The need for specific training in the area of disability for church volunteers is essential. Although two of the directors in the study first mentioned it was the heart of a person and their willingness to work with children with autism that was important, they both stated they would only put people who understood disabilities in charge of this ministry. It was clear from the observations, those who had more difficulty were those with less experience and training. However, training church volunteers when there are no training opportunities available at their church becomes a real problem. Church volunteers should be encouraged to read books on the subject. Among church volunteers there may be people who already work with children with disabilities that could serve as resources and provide training. Training for volunteers can come by networking with nearby universities or school districts. In addition, identifying nearby churches that have developed this ministry and learning from them is also an option. Two of the churches observed were very willing to have people come and observe their program.

Parents

All four of the parents interviewed for this study had very specific things to say about where their children should participate and how much they should participate. This is not uncommon, as all parents have to be advocates for their children with or without disabilities. What was interesting is that due to the parents not truly understanding their child's disability or not wanting to bother those caring for their children, they did not always ask the questions that needed to be asked to determine the best possible classroom and program for their child. Sam's father and Oscar's mother felt the need for a different approach for their child; however, neither one of them brought the issue up with church leaders. Although having to be an advocate for your own child can be difficult, it is quite necessary. In cases where there are absolutely no church programs and yet families want to stay at that church, they may have to bring up the topic of ministry programs for children with disabilities. They may also have to assist in developing such a ministry.

Overall Church Body

The church body needs to address negative attitudes, biases, and prejudice toward people with disabilities. Seeing people with disabilities as friends can help change these views. The idea of building friendships first is both expressed by Swinton (2011) and Hauerwas (2005). As members of the Body of Christ, it is the responsibility of Christians to change "attitudinal barriers" (Langer, 2012), regarding people with disabilities, in order for them to fully participate in the Body of Christ. Many times it may be these same "attitudinal barriers" that create an obstacle when attempting to welcome and accept children with autism. Churches need to respond to the need that is often being dismissed or neglected by being prepared to address the needs of children with autism and their families the minute those families show up at the door. That means that they have to have a plan in place as to how they will address this need even if there are currently no children with disabilities attending that church. The importance of how this affects the entire family cannot be overlooked.

In addition, as part of their values statement, the church needs to state how they will serve all populations. The idea of full inclusion even in the church seems to take over and people fail to realize churches actually serve other groups as separate groups. For example, most churches have a college ministry, a young married couples ministry, and a children's ministry. Some even have a ministry specifically for older adults. It should be recognized a disability ministry is also needed, even though some of the research that calls for full inclusion appears to see this as not including those with disabilities. To include people with disabilities does not simply mean to place them into already existing programs that may not serve their needs best, but it means developing specific programs that will.

Limitations

As with any study there are limitations. This study is a four-subject case study. The results and findings gathered are specific to these four cases; therefore, generalizations will be difficult to make. All of the children observed for this study were boys, further limiting the generalization of the findings. As there was only one researcher conducting the observations and interviews, the potential for researcher bias is high; however, to limit this bias the following steps were taken: careful observation notes, keeping journal notes, and member checking the data. Another limitation is the inability of a researcher to control bias from other adults. In at least one of the cases, it appeared some of the adult interaction with one of the children was influenced by the fact that an observer was present.

Recommendations for Future Research

This research study focused on the experiences of children with autism in the church. Through this study several questions arose regarding children with disabilities and should be explored further. With so many people with disabilities, why do churches not appear to have a plan to welcome people with disabilities? A survey polling churches on their knowledge and resources regarding ministry for people with disabilities may add to the existing research on this topic. This would help determine the barriers and challenges that arise at specific churches in an effort to provide support to address those barriers.

A second question to consider involves how public education is forming or influencing the way children with autism are being cared for in the church and if this influence is appropriate. The question came about in attempting to further understand how full inclusion was being presented in some churches and the push behind the strategy.

A third question is whether or not siblings of children with autism exhibit more empathy and compassion than children who grow up with typically developing siblings. In one case, the care that was observed from one of the siblings toward his brother with autism was significantly greater than observed in other children. When the question was posed to the mother whether this had been taught or expected of the sibling, she replied by saying that it was not. Whether this behavior was innate or learned could be further explored in another study.

Lastly, further research should address one of the main limitations of this research by taking this same study and replicating it with female children who have autism, to study if the interactions and experience of little girls with autism in the church would differ from the experiences of boys.

Conclusions

This study sought to further understand the experience of four boys with autism in an evangelical church in order to add to the existing research on the topic. By doing so, implications from this study were provided to various groups of people in the church: pastors, church volunteers, parents, and the overall church body. They ranged from offering specific resources, to imploring that the negative attitudes of those in the church be addressed. The specific recommendations also stated the importance of training. Without specific training for church volunteers on children with autism, churches cannot establish adequate ministries. The study concluded with stated limitations, as well as recommendations for future research.

References

Bailey, D. B., Golden, R. N., Roberts, J., & Ford, A. (2007). Maternal depression and developmental disability: Research critique. *Mental Retardation and Developmental Disabilities Research Reviews, 13*(4), 321-329.

Bennett, T., Deluca, D., & Bruns, D. (1997). Putting inclusion into practice: Perspectives of teachers and parents. *Exceptional Children, 64*(1) 115-131.

Brobst, J. B., Clopton, J. R., & Hendrick, S. S. (2009). Parenting children with autism spectrum disorders: The couples' relationship. *Focus on Autism & Other Developmental Disabilities, 24*(1), *38-49.*

Ceylan, R., & Aral, N. (2007). An examination of the correlation between depression and hopelessness levels in mothers of disabled children. *Social Behavior & Personality: An International Journal, 35*(7), 903-908.

Carlson, G. (2016). Guest editorial reaching those with special needs: Christian education and special needs ministry. *Christian Education Journal, Vol 13*, No. 1.

Gillham, B. (2000). *Case study research methods.* London: Continuum.

Gray, D. E. (2006). Coping over time: The parents of children with autism. *Journal of Intellectual Disability Research, 50*(12), 970-976.

Hartley, S. L., Barker, E. T., Seltzer, M. M., Greeberg, J., Bolt, D., Floyd, F., & Orsmond, G. (2010). The relative risk and timing of divorce in families of children with an autism spectrum disorder. *Journal of Family Psychology, (24)*4, 449-457.

Hauerwas, S. (2005). Chapter 1 Timeful friends. *Journal of Religion, Disability, & Health, 8*(3/4), 11-25.

Langer, R. (2011). The Body, the gifts, and the disabled. *The Magazine of the Evangelical Free*

Church of America. Retrieved from http://efcatoday.org/story/body-gifts-and-disabilities.

Lee, L., Harrington, R., Louie, B., & Newschaffer, C. (2008). Children with autism: Quality of life and parental concerns. *Journal of Autism and Developmental Disorders, 38*(6), 1147-1160.

Lewis, A. (2009). Methodological issues in exploring the ideas of children with autism concerning self and spirituality. *Journal of Religion, Disability, & Health, 13,* 64-74.

Newsome, W. S. (2000). Parental perceptions during periods of transition: Implications for social workers serving families coping with autism. *Journal of Family Social Work, 5*(2), 17-31.

Ramisch, J. L., Timm, T. M., Hock, R. M., & Topor, J. A. (2013). Experiences delivering a marital intervention for couples with children with autism spectrum disorder. *The American Journal of Family Therapy, 41,* 376-388.

Swinton, J. (2011). Who is the God we worship? Theologies of disability: Challenges and new possibilities. *International Journal of Practical Theology, 14*(2), 273-307.

Tarakeshwar, N., & Pargament, K. (2001). Religious coping in families of children with autism.

Author Biography

Dr. Uranga-Hernandez is an Associate Professor and Clinic Director at Biola University where she teaches at both the graduate and undergraduate levels in the Communication Sciences and Disorders Department. Her research interests include Multi-Cultural Issues, Autism, Language and Literacy Development and Disorders, early intervention, and Theology and Disabilities.

Special Needs Ministry Starts by Discovering the Needs of a Special Needs Family

Dr. Dave Kruse

When a person steps into a church, they should notice a variety of people. These people reflect the community in which the church resides. They represent different stages of life, different political views, different races, different socioeconomic levels, and different stages of spiritual maturity (Greear, 2016, p. 137). However, in some churches, there is a missing group. This group is a growing demographic in America, representing 18.7 percent of the United States population, yet it appears to be absent from most churches (Brault, 2012). This group is families with special needs children, specifically children with mental, emotional, and physical disabilities. While some churches have a Special Needs Ministry, it appears most churches are not actively seeking to engage this group or even aware they are missing from the congregation.

When the church is aware of this group, many times the church does not understand how it can engage them. This group's unique needs can be intimidating to a church with limited resources. Rather than seek to engage these families, the church ignores them. However, this is not how it should be. Churches should seek to engage all people, no matter the challenge they bring, in the life of the church. Rather than view special needs families as a burden to avoid, churches should view these families as an opportunity to demonstrate what it means to love all people and potentially grow God's kingdom. However, to engage special needs families, churches need to understand that special needs families have similar needs as typical families in regard to participating in the life of the church, but they express those needs in different ways. As churches understand the challenges special needs families face in participating in the life of the church, the church is better able to respond to the various types of special needs in their congregation and community, allocate resources to minister to these families, and possibly redefine what the church considers ministry success.

In an effort to encourage churches to start special needs ministry, the researcher focused his doctoral project on devising a strategy to include families with special needs children in the Sunday morning activities at his church. This involved establishing a theological foundation for special needs ministry, discovering the needs of families with special needs children in regard to their participation in church, observing existing special needs ministries, and devising and refining the strategy. While the strategy is unique to his church, the theological foundations, research process, and findings on the needs of families with special needs are common for all churches.

Let Us Make Man in Our Image (Genesis 1:26–27)

Any ministry effort should stand on theology. An understanding of God's heart for all people allows for an understanding of God's heart for people with special needs. Throughout Scripture, God shows His heart for people with special needs. While a complete study of Scripture is beyond the scope of this article, Genesis 1 provides a foundational truth when ministering to people with special needs. In Genesis 1, Moses shares God's creative work that culminates in the creation of man in His image, also known as *Imago Dei*. The *Imago Dei* found in all people confers dignity, entrusts responsibility, and implants the capacity to mirror the Creator (Walton, 2001, p. 137). As such, the creation of man in God's image has great implications on the intrinsic value of all people.

There are three prominent views about how *Imago Dei* manifests itself in man and how one's understanding of the image affects how one treats others and ministers to them (Erickson, 1998, pp. 518-519). The substantive view says the image is some definite characteristic or quality within the human makeup (Erickson, 1998, pp. 520-521). Within the substantive view, there exist many different focuses, but each focus points towards the position of the image. The *Imago Dei* is a quality given by God and all people have it, even if they do not believe in God (Erickson, 1998, pp. 522-523). The substantive view tries to identify the characteristics and mannerisms of man that mimic the characteristics and mannerisms of God. Though an exhaustive list of similarities between God and man is not possible, Grudem (1994) notes the image of God manifests itself in every person in his or her moral, spiritual, mental, relational, and physical aspects (p. 450).

Unlike the substantive view, the relational view does not ask questions about the nature of humans. Instead of the characteristics and mannerisms of man reflecting *Imago Dei*, the relational view holds the relationship and experiences between man and God defines *Imago Dei*. Because of the focus of the relational view, the *Imago Dei* becomes dynamic and not static (Erickson, 1998, p. 526). The relational view looks for the *Imago Dei* as men and women interact with God and other people. The third view, called the functional view, views the image as something one does, most often expressed as man's dominion over the creation (Erickson, 1998, p. 527). Rather than the characteristics of people or the relationships held between people as the expression of *Imago Dei*, the functional views holds the actions of man show the image of God.

Though all three views have weaknesses, Erickson (1998) holds the substantive view as the most complete way to view the image of God found in man (p. 532). The image is in the very nature of humans, refers to what humans are, and is not dependent upon the functions of man. Simply by being human, one bears the image of God (Erickson, 1998, p. 532). Because the nature of man contains the image of God, all people bear God's image, which imparts value and worth. The ability of a person to perform a function or establish certain types of relationship does not affect *Imago Dei*.

Understanding the theology of *Imago Dei* leads to an understanding of the value of all people (Hokema, 1986, p. 78). Since God made every person in His image, every person represents and reflects God. Grudem (1994) says man is the culmination of God's creative work, and though marred by sin, we reflect much of His image and shall grow in Christlikeness (p. 450). God chose all people to bear His image, which imparts dignity to all people. How the church views the dignity of people affects how the church responds to people's needs (Walton, 2001, p. 138). The church that understands the theology of *Imago Dei* hopefully sees all people as valuable and worthy of inclusion in the life of the church. The Bible clearly displays God's heart for those with a disability (Beys, 2016). To exclude a person or family from participating in the life of the church because they look or act differently, or their actions or appearance make others uncomfortable, contradicts the heart of God.

The Research Methodology

Upon understanding God's heart for people with special needs, the project director began researching and developing a strategy for special needs ministry at his church. The project director began by determining his church had a need for a special needs ministry using a survey of families at the church. The survey was anonymous and had several purposes. First, the survey sought to identify the type of special needs currently represented at the church. Second, the survey sought to obtain the parents view on the current state of special needs ministry at the church. Last, the survey provided parents opportunity to share how the church could better minister to them and their child with special needs.

Upon determining the need for a special needs ministry, the project director undertook several steps. First, the project director explored various models of special needs ministry. This involved reading books, articles, and other literature that focused on special needs ministry models and the unique needs of special needs families. Second, the project director interviewed three churches that had established special needs ministry. The project director chose each church for a specific reason. Church A had recently started their special needs ministry. This allowed the project director to hear the challenges they faced starting the new ministry and how they addressed each challenge. Church B was similar size to the project director's church. This allowed the project director to develop an understanding of what special needs ministry could look like at his church with similar resources. Church C was larger than the project director's church and represented what could be if the project director's church embraced ministering to families with special needs. Each church provided insight into how their special needs ministry started, how the ministry functioned, how the churches recruited and trained leaders, and any thoughts they had for a church starting a special needs ministry. Along with these interviews, throughout the project, the project director found himself having conversations with parents, teachers, special needs ministers, therapists, and others who interact with people with special needs. Though most of these conversations were not specifically ministry focused, each conversation influenced the direction of the strategy.

Third, the project director attended a special needs ministry seminar offered by Rising Above Ministries that focused on helping churches start a special needs ministry. The seminar addressed common misconceptions on the difficulty of starting a special needs ministry and practical steps to start a special needs ministry. Fourth, the project director devised a strategy for including families with special needs children in the Sunday morning activities at his church. The project director took the information gained from the survey, research, and interviews to devise a strategy specifically for the culture at his church. Though the strategy addresses the specifics for the project director's church, the framework of the strategy is viable for many church settings. Last, the project director utilized an expert panel to revise the strategy to its final state. The expert panel included a teacher with special needs certification, the President of Rising Above Ministries, who is also a father of a son with special needs, and the special needs minister at one of the interviewed churches. At the completion of the project, the project director submitted the strategy to the leadership of his church for consideration to implement in the near future.

Findings

While some may prefer seeing the details of the project director's strategy, understanding the factors that influenced the formation of the strategy is valuable. These factors are common to any special needs family. The findings of the project served to determine the strategy for a special needs ministry at the project director's church. The following details are large findings that pertain to any special needs ministry, not just ministry at the project director's church.

The Needs of Special Needs Families

Any family attending a church brings with them a set of needs they hope the church can meet. However, the requirements of the special needs family may include needs not found in a typical family or their needs require greater intentional response on the part of the church. The needs of both the typical and special needs families may be similar in nature, but the response to the special needs family may require unique elements not required by a typical family. Through a survey of special needs families at his church, interviews with churches with special needs ministries, and the research and thoughts of other authors, the project director identified five needs common to special needs families as they attempt to join in the life of a local congregation (Hubach, 2006).

Acceptance/Inclusion

Attempting to define acceptance presents a challenge because it means many things to many people. At the heart of understanding acceptance is the concept of belonging. By looking the same as those in the church, acting the way they do, going to the places they go, listening to the same music, and dressing the same way as the majority, it is easy for one to feel like they belong. For a special needs family, blending in is usually not possible. Their child is different in the way they look, act, or move. The differences a special needs family carries with them challenges the idea that acceptance is blending in and requires churches to examine what does it mean for people to belong and be accepted. The key to acceptance in the church is understanding that the church is a collection of unique people, all created in the image of God, with different personalities, strengths, weaknesses, needs, and gifts. Rather than expecting the people in the church to be the same, the church should seek to embrace the differences in people that make them unique and bring diversity to the body of Christ.

However, this is not always the case for churches. Instead of embracing people different from them, they seek to keep the norm and maintain a sense of balance and control in the life of the church. When someone who is different—be that a difference of skin color, political views, or ability—tries to join in the life of the church, they may find they are not accepted. Rather than encountering acceptance, those who are different may discover tolerance at best and exclusion at worst (Conference of Catholic Bishops, 2013). Acceptance is more than simply allowing a person's presence. It is the act of bringing them into the life of the church, inviting them to participate in the ministry of the church, and the church assuming the responsibility to walk with them on their faith journey. The survey of families with special needs at the project director's church provides a wide range of attitudes toward the church's acceptance of their child and family. On one side, Family 5, a family whose daughter has Spina Bifida, said the church could not love their daughter more and they made her feel special. On the other side, Family 4, a family whose son has autism, commented the church needs to adopt a mindset for special needs children and love their child for who they are (Kruse, 2017, p. 133). Each family attends the same church but has experienced different acceptance of their child's special needs. A church that desires to minister to families with special needs must instill a culture that accepts people with special needs as willingly as they accept a person without special needs.

Worship

Worship is the act of praising and exalting God (Erickson, 1998, p. 1066) and is the reason God created humanity (Westminster Catechism, 1647). The greatest thing man and woman can do is worship God. When a Christian worships God, they do so with their whole self—they adore God with their heart, praise Him with their voice, and speak so others hear (Grudem, 1994, p. 1003). The act of worship is twofold in practice. First, it is a personal act. Worship is an individual responding to God with their entire being. He or she is able to worship God no matter their location because God is with them at all times. For men and women who are Christians, they are capable of worshiping God anywhere if they engage worship with their head and heart. Christians should seek private time with God through prayer, reading Scripture, fasting, and other acts of worship.

A believer's private worship time prepares them for the second practice of worship, the corporate act of worshiping. Throughout the Old Testament, the nation of Israel comes together to worship God. In Exodus 24, Moses and the elders of Israel worshiped God. In Nehemiah 9, Israel gathered to confess their sins and worship God. King Josiah, in 2 Kings 22, called on all the elders to hear the Law, respond to it, and worship God. In the New Testament, the church in Acts 2 gathered day-by-day to worship God. Worship is a corporate activity that places believers in close proximity with one another to participate together in the intimate act of ascribing glory and praise to God, to interceding for one another before the throne of the God, and to forge bonds of shared experience in the presence of their King. Hubach (2006) describes corporate worship as a corporate response to the gospel where the parts of the body praise and exalt God for His character and work in the lives of believers. Worship, practiced individually and corporately, is valuable in the life of all Christians.

Families with special needs children also need to worship with their church on a regular basis. However, in most congregations it is not easy to find families with special needs children consistently attending worship (Kessler Foundation and National Organization on Disability, 2010, p. 129). The project director's research found a variety of responses from special needs families as they considered worship. Ault, Collins, and Carter (2013) found that 56 percent of parents with special needs children had prevented their child from participating in religious activities because of a lack of support. In the survey of special needs families at the project director's church, Family 1, a family whose son has severe developmental coordination disorder, sensory processing disorder, and several other delays and disorders, shared they do not attend worship service because sitting through it is very hard (Kruse, 2017, p. 133). Other families do not worship together as one parent must stay with their special needs child while the other parent attends a worship service (J. Davidson, personal communication, March 9, 2016). Another option families may choose involves families choosing to participate in portions of the service with their special needs child and leave during the portions when their child may cause a disruption (A. Mylam, personal communication, May 12, 2016). Families with special needs children face a tension when they try to worship with their church family. They value worship but are either tired and stressed out and do not want to face another challenge or they are concerned about disrupting the service and bothering other believers. If worship is the chief end of man, then churches should seek methods to include families with special needs children in worship. This does not mean elevating the person with special needs above typical people when designing a worship service. It means considering if there is opportunity for the person with special needs to corporately participate in worship. If the church and family decide together a person's needs are so great that they prevent him or her from participating in a corporate worship service, the church ought to respond with appropriate care for the person with special needs so his or her family may participate in a worship service. When families with special needs children are not able to worship, they do not experience the dynamic of corporate worship that many believers take for granted.

Community/Support

At the heart of humans is the desire to know and be known. First, to know and be known by God. Second, to know and be known by other people. Bill Donahue and Russ Robinson (2001) share God created humans for dependence on Him, interdependence with Him, and communal interdependence within the church (p. 37). When a person participates in a community of believers, they gain strength, wisdom, accountability, and acceptance (Donahue and Robinson, 2001, p. 38). As believers share grace with one another, bonds of trust and unity form allowing them to share the joys and pains of life with one another. In most churches, community forms between believers through Sunday school and other small group ministries. Through the relationships formed in these groups, people are known and know others.

Churches that do not offer special needs ministry manage to exclude many families with special needs children from small groups. In the project director's church survey, Family 2, a family whose son has autism, said there is no class equipped to handle their son's special needs and thus the parents are unable to participate in discipleship groups on Sunday, social events, or Bible studies offered during the week (Kruse, 2017, p. 132). Similar to participating in worship, families are not able to attend a group when there are no options of care or participation for their child with special needs. In these situations, the parents, other siblings, and special needs children miss community with others within the church. However, parents with special needs children look to their church family for support, encouragement, and a place to share their struggles and joys (Bolduc, 2001, p. 24). Community allows families with special needs children to know other people and for them to be known by others in the church. Churches that desire community for all the people in the church should take into consideration the challenges special needs families face in establishing relationships that provide them community (Carter, 2007, pp. 29-30).

Discipleship

Discipleship is the process of believers learning about God and His mission and adjusting their lives to line up with what they learn and know about God. It is more than Bible study within the confines of a small group, though that is part of discipleship. Discipleship, in the context of a local congregation, happens when acceptance exists and community develops. When acceptance and community form between believers, the relationships naturally move into discipleship. Discipleship apart from the context of a church allows only for the development of a personal relationship with God. Discipleship within the context of a local congregation allows for the development of a personal relationship with God and an understanding of how a person fits within the body of Christ.

Discipleship with families who have children, be they special needs children or not, has two focuses. The first focus is discipleship of the children. Families seek churches that engage their children with the truth found in the Bible, provide an environment that is both engaging and safe, and that care about the well-being of the family. The second focus is discipleship of the parents. Parents seeking to raise children that love God with all of themselves need discipleship so they may point their children toward God in their day-to-day family life.

In order for churches to include families with special needs children in their discipleship ministry, churches must evaluate their current discipleship efforts. Many churches hesitate to adjust their discipleship ministry for children with special needs because they feel it will take a lot of resources and effort. Hubach (2006) encourages churches to make the adjustment because the effort is not as much as they anticipate (p. 35). Organizations like Rising Above Ministries exist to help churches adjust their current programs to include children with special needs. By including children with special needs in classrooms with their typical peers, the church is communicating love and acceptance to the family (Bolduc, 2001, p. 25).

Contribution

God gives all of His people gifts and abilities for advancing His Kingdom. In 1 Corinthians 12, Paul talks about various spiritual gifts found in the body of Christ. God gives spiritual gifts to His followers so they may serve; there is an expectation that all church members will exercise and use their gifts to fulfill the vision and mission of the church. There is no mandate that only those who are fully abled will contribute to the ministry of the church. Nor is there an exemption for those whose family includes a special needs member. There may be limitations to their ability to participate but the church that values special needs families will seek opportunities for them to contribute to the ministry of the church. When a church ministers to special needs children, they provide opportunity for the rest of the family to contribute and serve. Hubach (2006) points out that many times the focus on special needs people is their inability and their ability is overlooked. Bolduc (2001), a mother of special needs son, feels most special needs parents want their children to contribute to the ministry of the church (p. 25). In their interview with the project director, Church A shared they involve their special needs teenagers in the ministry of the church each week during the second service by having them do a project that benefits one of the ministries of the church (Kruse, 2017, p. 120). Some projects focused on stuffing envelopes, putting together visitor bags, and drawing pictures/writing cards of encouragement for various church members. Churches that value all people will seek ways to allow children with special needs to discover their spiritual gifts and opportunities to exercise them in the life of the church.

Summary

The thought of starting a special needs ministry may be daunting to many churches. The thought of finding enough leaders, creating space in the budget, and potential disruptions that may accompany a family with special needs are all factors that may keep a church from starting a special needs ministry. The key to overcoming the initial hesitation involves understanding God's heart for all people, including people with special needs. A church reflecting the heart of God should desire to overcome the challenges and objections to starting a special needs ministry. With time, research, reaching out to those with experience ministering to people with special needs, and perseverance, a church should find they are capable of welcoming, loving, and connecting with special needs families. As special needs families experience acceptance, have opportunity to worship, and grow in their faith at a local church, they bring their unique abilities and gifts to the church. As special needs families and the local church come together, the body of Christ becomes more complete, the Kingdom of God grows, and God is glorified!

References

Ault, M. J., Collins, B. C., & Carter, E. W. (2013, February). Congregational participation and support for children and adults with disabilities. *Intellectual and Developmental Disabilities*, 51, 48-61.

Beys, R. (2015). A biblical view of disability. *BeThinking*. Retrieved December 15, 2016, from http://www.bethinking.org/human-life/a-biblical-view-of-disability.

Bolduc, K. (2010). *A place called acceptance: Ministry with families of children with disabilities*. Louisville, KY: Bridge Resources.

Brault, M. (2012, July). Current Population Reports. *Americans with Disabilities: 2010. Household Economics Study, P70-131*. Retrieved February 26, 2016, from https://www2.census.gov/library/publications/2012/demo/p70-131.pdf

Carter, E. W. (2007). *Including people with disabilities in faith communities*. Baltimore, MD: Paul H. Brooks Publishing Co.

Donahue, B., & Robinson, R. (2001). *Building a church of small groups: A place where nobody stands alone*. Grand Rapids, MI: Zondervan.

Erickson, M. J. (1998). *Christian Theology* (2nd ed.). Grand Rapids, MI: Baker.

Greear, J. (2016, July 20). Plumb Line #9: We Should Reflect the Diversity of Our Community and Proclaim the Diversity of the Kingdom. *J. D. Greear Blog*. Retrieved January 27, 2017, from http://www.jdgreear.com/my_weblog/2016/07/plumb-line-9-we-should-reflect-the-diversity-of-our-community-proclaim-the-diversity-of-the-kingdom.html.

Grudem, W. (1994). *Systematic Theology: An introduction to biblical doctrine*. Grand Rapids, MI: Zondervan.

Hoekema, A. A. (1986). *Created in God's image.* Grand Rapids, MI: Eerdman's.

Hubach, S. (2006). *Same lake, different boat: Coming alongside people touched by disability.* Phillipsburg, NJ: P&R Publishing.

Kessler Foundation and National Organization on Disability. (2010). *The ADA 20 years later: Kessler Foundation/NOD survey of americans with disabilities.* Retrieved December 28, 2016, from https://www.nod.org/downloads/best-practices/07c_2010_survey_of_americans_with_disabilities_gaps_full_report.pdf.

Kruse, D. (2017). *Developing a strategy to include families with special needs children in the Sunday morning activities at Stevens Street Baptist Church* (Doctor of Ministry thesis). Retrieved from Proquest Dissertations and Theses database. (UMI No. 10274432).

United States Conference of Catholic Bishops (2013). *Pastoral statement of U.S. Catholic Bishops on people with disabilities: Including the 1988 resolution on the tenth anniversary of the pastoral statement on persons with disabilities.* Washington D.C.: United States Conference of Catholic Bishops.

Walton, J. (2001). *The NIV Application Commentary: Genesis.* Grand Rapids, MI: Zondervan.

Author Biography

David B. Kruse, D.Min. has over 15 years-experience ministering to teenagers and their families. He and his wife are the proud parents of a son with autism.

The Church's Role in Educating Children Living in Poverty

Dr. Dena Moten

Introduction

The effects of poverty on education have been a topic of discussion for generations. Extensive research has been conducted that seeks to determine the link between children born into low-socioeconomic (SES) communities and their capacity to achieve academically. Both educational and governmental entities have sought to provide resolutions to what some have called a social epidemic.

> As the 1960s dawned, the postwar prosperity had eluded a large section of the population. The President's Council of Economic Advisors estimated that nearly 20% of the nation's population lived in poverty in 1962. President Lyndon B. Johnson believed that the government should play a more extensive role in reducing poverty and introduced legislation to expend social welfare programs in a number of areas, including education. (Lynch, 2016)

Not only have proposed solutions been offered by the government, but the religious community has served low-SES families. Whether through providing food and/or housing assistance, life skills training, or tutorial programs, numerous pastors and congregations recognize the necessity to serve the underprivileged, particularly when many churches are in or nearby impoverished neighborhoods. While churches who serve low-SES families must be commended, this article suggests that Scripture offers a biblical *mandate*, which outlines how Christians must view our role in the lives of the poor; for congregations whose objective is educational enrichment to poverty-stricken areas, this author advocates for and describes how ancillary programs can integrate educational methodologies into their instruction.

Yet, for the Christian educator, more far-reaching than the educational methodologies must be God's view of the mind and the teacher's responsibility to understand how it informs learning and teaching.

> To the Christian, the mind is understood as the sum total of all a person's conscious state which includes our thoughts, memories, feelings, and emotions. The brain allows for variety in how each person synthesizes ideas, argues an issue, or expresses a mood. However, when the brain is off, the mind is off! (Koh, 1993, p. 3)

This paper will explain the necessity for individuals who provide academic instruction in Christian organizations to have knowledge of the relationship between brain function and cognitive development in, especially, low-SES children. The oft-referenced authority Eric Jensen describes the process this way:

> The human brain 'downloads' the environment indiscriminately in an attempt to understand and absorb the surrounding world, whether that world is positive or negative. Behavior research shows that children from impoverished homes develop psychiatric disturbances and maladaptive social functioning at a greater rate than their affluent counterparts do. (Jensen, 2009, p. 17)

For this reason, Christian educators who instruct low-SES students must put forth a concerted effort to stay abreast of current findings in education that will empower them to reach *all* students and lead them to success. King David speaks to this in Psalms 139:13 (NASB), "For You [God] formed my inward parts; You wove me in my mother's womb;" therefore, Christians who teach children in any capacity have a responsibility to educate themselves on how the brain, created by God, should guide instruction.

> . . . the brain is viewed as more than an anatomical organ. It is a marvelous organ created by God (Genesis 1). It is a complex organ that directs and interprets our sensations, thinking, reactions,

evaluations, and helps us to discriminate right from wrong, good from bad. (Koh, 1993, p. 2)

How then is *poverty* defined among children? According to the American Community Survey (ACS), "If a family's total income is less than the dollar value of the appropriate threshold, then that family and every individual in it are considered to be in poverty. Similarly, if an unrelated individual's total income is less than the appropriate threshold, then that individual is considered to be in poverty" (Poverty Tract, 2015). For example, in 2015 the weighted average threshold for a unit containing four persons equaled $24,257; when two of the individuals in the unit are related children under 18 years of age, the poverty threshold was calculated at $24,036 (Poverty Thresholds, 2016). When referencing schools specifically, the National Center for Education Statistics defines *high poverty schools* as having "more than 75% of the students qualify for free or reduced-priced lunch" ("The Condition of Education," 2015).

It is important to mention that, for the author, a family's income level having a direct correlation to a child's performance can be verified beyond the research. Having worked in many capacities in low-income neighborhoods and schools, students struggling on end-of-grade tests, being plagued with suspensions, and often performing below grade level is the impetus for the author's examination into the topic. Supporting low-SES communities means being privy to the effects of not only academic gaps but both cognitive and social shortfalls.

Eric Jensen (2009) corroborates the writer's observation in *Teaching with Poverty in Mind* stating,

> The cognitive stimulation parents provide in the early childhood years is crucial, and as we have seen, poor children receive less of it than their well-off peers do. These deficits have been linked to underdeveloped cognitive, social, andemotional competence in later childhood and have shown to be increasingly important influences on vocabulary growth, IQ, and social skills. (p. 38)

For the professional educator or volunteer in an ancillary educational facility, such as a church tutorial or after-school community program, witnessing the low-SES student struggle academically is troubling; not being able to document a significant change after months of teaching and tutoring is both discouraging and disheartening. Research reveals when teachers, whether professional or lay, commit to broaden their knowledge of the teaching profession, one's ability to affect change increases. Wilson and Conyers (2013) state, "…teachers have greater opportunities than they had previously to test the different strategies and lessons, constantly enhancing their skills and experiencing the thrill of seeing their students gain in understanding" (p. 27). For Christians who educate children in any capacity, expanding one's ability in the field of education begins with understanding the following biblical mandate.

A Biblical Mandate

Nicole Baker Fulgham, author of *Educating All God's Children* states, "Every Christian has a duty to protect human beings from systemic injustice whenever and wherever we can. Examples throughout the Old Testament illustrate God's desire to eliminate unequal structures" (p. 107). For example, God gave instruction to the children of Israel in Exodus 23:10-11 in how servants should be treated in the Sabbath year to ensure they enjoy equal benefits from the food produced by the land. "For six years you shall sow your land and gather in its yield, but the seventh year you shall let it rest and lie fallow, that the poor of your people may eat; …" (ESV). Clarke's Commentary provides the following explanations for this command:

> To maintain as far as possible an equality of condition among the people, in setting the slaves at liberty, and in permitting all, as children of one family, to have the free and indiscriminate use of whatever the earth produced; to inspire the people with sentiments of humanity, by making it their duty to give rest, and proper and sufficient nourishment, to the poor, the slave, and the stranger, and even to the cattle. (GodVine, 2017)

Again, in Deuteronomy 24, God gave special consideration to women, who at that time, were subordinates in society. When husband and wife found reason to separate under the law, God commanded there be a "writ of divorce" as a means of protection for the woman who was often demeaned and disgraced. "Divorce as permitted in the Mosaic Law because of the hardness of the Israelites' hearts, endangered the dignity of women within the theocracy. Hence, easy abuse of the permission was forestalled by circumscribing it with technicalities and restrictions (Deut. 24:1-4) (Pfeiffer, 1962, p. 188).

The New Testament also provides instructions regarding the care of those living in poverty. In Luke 3:11, John instructs his listeners "Whoever has two tunics is to share with him who has none, and whoever has food is to do likewise" (ESV). "The response John gives to the crowd is not complicated or impossible, for a heart that has been truly turned towards God is one that desires to meet the needs of others" (Brock, 1994, p. 309). When considering the above Scriptures, extending oneself to children in poverty should become a priority for Christians.

Finally, in Jeremiah 7:5-7, God used the prophet Jeremiah to express to Judah how they must alter their ways to enter the land of promise. God's commands include applying justice to society's feeble, which includes children. The passage reads,

> . . . if you truly practice justice between a man and his neighbor, *if* you do not oppress the alien, the orphan, or the widow, and do not shed innocent blood in this place, nor walk after other gods to your own ruin, then I will let you dwell in this place, and in the land that I gave to your fathers forever and ever. (NASB)

Moreover, Christian educators possess not only biblical faith, but a knowledge of God where the complexities of human development are understood in light of Him as Creator. It is this knowledge that reinforces the Christian's responsibility to handle children with the understanding that they are "fearfully and wonderfully" made by God. "Scripture tells us that we are fearfully and wonderfully made, and this insight applies to the *soul* as well as the *body*" (Moreland, 1997, p. 72). Again, Christian teachers share a clear distinction from others, as we have the authority, through the power of the Holy Spirit, to effect change in the lives of low-SES children on multiple levels. One level being the "command center" for the *body* or what some refer to as the most intricate and mysterious organ created. Jensen (2005) shares that, "the brain is much more than an anatomical structure, it is also an active processing center, always at work" (p. 8).

Those in faith communities who serve children from low-SES communities bring into the instructional setting a scriptural directive that forces one to view students as body (including the brain), soul (including the element that can be redeemed), and spirit (including the aspect that can commune with God) and more than just recipients of information. Moreland (1996) asserts:

> Seen as a discipline, study becomes a means of building my character, ingraining habits of thoughts and reflection, and reinforcing in my own soul the value of the life of the mind. We study, then, not simply to gain knowledge about the topic of study but as a broader spiritual discipline. (p. 112)

The Effects of Socio-economics on Education

The expectation for students in a learning environment is to enter the classroom focused and prepared to learn. Unless the pupil has been identified as having academic challenges, teachers assume students can effectively manage learning opportunities and interactions with peers. Because of what many low-SES students experience both in their homes and before arriving to the classroom, meeting this expectation is not possible.

> Each child has a limited set of internal resources for dealing with everyday worries as well as bigger stressors. Once that capacity is maxed out, the first casualty is school. Why? When kids are worried about being evicted or living in abusive households, doing well in school barely makes it onto the to-do list. If you have a painful, persistent toothache, the teacher's well-designed lesson seems irrelevant. To get kids to focus on academic excellence, we must remove the real-world concerns that are much higher on their mental and emotional priority lists. (Jensen, 2009, p. 73)

Having taught and counseled with children from a range of socioeconomic backgrounds, this writer understands that academic challenges and diminished cognitive function do not discriminate between wealthy families and those in poverty. But what distinguishes the two groups is accessibility. Children who enjoy middle to upper class lifestyles often have the advantage of parents who have earned college degrees, provided children with regular doctor visits, tutors, and other educational programs that serve to bridge the cognitive gap a child might experience. Jensen (2009) stated, "Poor children have fewer and less-supportive networks than their more affluent counterparts do; live in neighborhoods that are lower in social capital; and, as adolescents, are more likely to rely on peers than on adults for social and emotional support" (p. 8). According to many behaviorists, these children are not capable of advancing beyond what they are introduced to in their surroundings, and when they are placed in a more progressive environment than what their exposure has allowed, they will undoubtedly struggle in their new space.

> "It has been said that the modern person is exposed to more stimuli in a 24-hour period than medieval man was exposed to in his entire lifetime. Therefore, one must be equipped with the tools required in order to decide upon and differentiate among numerous and almost overwhelming options" (Feuerstein, Feuerstein, and Faulk, 2010, p. 1).

For individuals with underdeveloped cognitive abilities, when abruptly taken out of one social class and placed in another, the plethora of options now available *can* result in destructive behavior.

Methodologies

Jensen (2009) defined *poverty* as "a chronic and debilitating condition that results from multiple adverse synergistic risk factors and affect the mind, body, and soul" (p. 6). He explained the necessity for those in the field of education to understand the needs of students who are faced daily with poverty's ill-effects. "Poverty, calls for key information and smarter strategies, not resignation and despair" (Jensen, 2009, p. 5). While many educational strategies can be convoluted, especially for the novice educator or church volunteer, it is the objective of this author to simplify two practices for use in most programs with proper training.

Mediated Learning Experience

Reuven Feuerstein, developed Mediated Learning Experience (MLE) and Structural Cognitive Modifiability (SCM) based on his work with children of the Holocaust. Arguing against the theory of fixed intelligence, Feuerstein contends that MLE can foster a student's ability to adapt to their environment thus creating new brain structures and increasing cognitive functions. From this research, he authored *Beyond Smarter*, detailing how MLE and SCM can help even the most disadvantaged children learn.

While working with families of Holocaust survivors in 1944 and 1945, Professor Feuerstein was given the responsibility of educating physically worn and emotionally damaged

children who immigrated to what was then Palestine. Knowing they had experienced traumatic life events, Feuerstein's objective was to interrupt their emotionally disturbed pasts, steering them toward unfamiliar but productive ways of learning and experiencing their environments.

Feuerstein (2010) found that MLE can expand a student's cognitive function and involves three elements that aid the adult mediator in building a child's thinking processes. According to Feuerstein, the mediator must be *intentional* with the learner reciprocating what is being taught; the mediator must give the stimulus of focus *meaning*, and finally, the learner should develop skills to use what has been acquired in varying situations or what Feuerstein calls *transcendence*.

Accompanying MLE is SCM, which is defined as the alteration of a human's cognitive function as a result of receiving guidance on how to respond to external stimuli. Feuerstein (2010) refers to SCM as the "theory and application of MLE" (p. 23). Applying a single definition to SCM is problematic, as Feuerstein (2010) gives several examples of how the concept applies.

> One of the central assumptions of the theory of structural cognitive modifiability (SCM) is expressed in the quality of creating structural change, according to which a human being is both adaptive and unpredictable. When the change that occurs is liable to continue beyond what it was in the beginning, the capacity to change structurally turns the human being into an entity about whom neither the manner in which it will continue to exist nor the direction of

its development can be predicted. This is the quality of adaptability and self-perpetuation. (pp. 13-14)

Structural Change

One's ability to adapt will over time increase his or her capacity for learning and modify performance. Structural change affords one the skill to move beyond temporary modifications often found in tutoring and "teaching the test" to permanent changes in cognitive function. "Change that is structural will affect learning and behavior in deep, sustaining, and self-perpetuating ways" (Feuerstein, 2010, p. 13). The continuous adaptability of one's behavior and aptitude for learning makes SCM vital to a child's future judgment, reasoning, and decision-making skills. For any child whose conduct and cognition have been shaped by unfavorable influences, introducing him or her to MLE can result in meaningful and constructive cognitive and behavioral changes. These cognitive developments allow the child with limited experiences to relate to and understand life outside of his or her immediate setting. "We differentiate those types of changes, which give a different character to their experiences and enable the understanding of their experiences, from changes that lead one to interact with the world differently than what had been previously experienced" (Feuerstein, 2010, p. 7).

Jensen (2009), who wrote extensively on the topic of educating children living in poverty, created the acronym SHARE to direct schools and educational facilities on how to best serve low-SES students. This author maintains that joining Feuerstein's MLE (intentionality, meaning, transcendence) with Jensen's SHARE, will over time, produce cognitively competent students.

High Expectations

It is vital for pastors, youth ministers, teachers, etc., to understand that despite the socioeconomic status of the students being served, setting high expectations for learners is imperative; in many cases, the demand for high achievement by educators is what attracts parents to a particular program. But one must be aware of what "high expectations" *do not* look like for many low-SES children. "School leaders who adopt the mantra of high expectations often demand that their students sit quietly, remain attentive, show motivation, stay out of trouble, work hard, and act polite ..." (Jensen, 2009, p. 69). According to Jensen, expecting the above from most students living in poverty is unrealistic. He states, "those students are in fact hungry, unhealthy, stressed, and emotionally stretched to the edge" (p. 69). Yet, fusing SHARE and MLE can be life-changing for a child, as eventually, marked changes will be observed in behavior and cognitive function.

"SHARE"
- **S**upport the Whole Child
- **H**ard Data
- **A**ccountability
- **R**elationship Building
- **E**nrichment Mind-Set (p. 69)

Support the Whole Child

While high academic achievement for low-SES students is certainly possible to attain, schools, enrichment centers, after-school programs, etc. must first meet the child's basic needs. Without having these basics satisfied, expecting students to be motivated to learn is irrational. "Until your school finds ways to address the social, emotional, and health-related challenges that your kids face every day, academic excellence is just a politically correct but highly unlikely goal" (Jensen, 2009, p. 70).

> To understand why these services are needed, we must go back more than half a century to Abraham Maslow's (1943) hierarchy of needs, which asserts that students cannot be expected to function at a high academic level when their basic needs—for food, shelter, medical care, safety, family, and friendships, for example— are unmet. (Jensen, 2009, p. 70)

For the organization with limited resources, one must engage parishioners and/or members of the community to access their areas of expertise. It may be necessary to evaluate your student population to gauge the immediate needs. Jensen (2009) maintains that "kids who get wraparound support are able to stop dwelling on their problems and limitations and start focusing on the educational opportunities available to them" (p. 70).

Hard Data

In most cases, church tutorial programs do not administer standardized testing. This is where establishing a relationship with the child's school and teacher is imperative. A structured schedule of volunteer staff who have developed relationships with parents and teachers should be initiated to gather academic data and learning styles. One must interpret the data considering MLE and SCM—standardized tests are an indication of the child's current learning capacity and does not indicate *fixed* intelligence. "The result of various interrelation of human shaping environments and environments shaping humans is that there is no fixed human brain; it is always a work in progress" (Jensen, 2005, p. 11).

Accountability

All too often, volunteers in church auxiliaries and/or community organizations dismiss the need for accountability. After all, "We're working for free!" Specifically, concerning the church, accountability must originate with leadership. After fashioning a clear mission for one's enrichment program, pastors should communicate the mission and expectations to those serving in the program. Next, parents must be accountable to the teachers and to the mission of the organization; students must also be accountable to their instructors. "The best way to achieve accountability is to create a compelling, collaborative goal and then to administer formative assessments that provide useful, specific date demonstrating progress toward that goal" (Jensen, 2005, p. 80). As mentioned previously, while data can be obtained from the student's school, volunteer staff can evaluate students using electronic assessments.

Relationship Building

Building relationships with children living in low-SES settings is essential. In many cases, children in families plagued with impoverished conditions fail to form meaningful relationships for various reasons; therefore, the associations formed outside of family become particularly meaningful. It is in these relationships that students will experience MLE, as staff who have been trained in the methodology will find the opportunity to intentionally bring meaning to a stimulus of interest to the child, with the goal of seeing the student transcend or use what has been taught in diverse situations.

> Although strong student-parent relationships are ideal, students often seek out and value relationships with teachers, counselors, and mentors. Teachers who are sensitive to their students and who openly share their enthusiasm for learning and their belief in their students' abilities can help buffer low-SES kids from many risks and stressors they experience in their lives. (Jensen, 2009, p. 88)

Jensen (2009) explains that in addition to the teacher-student relationship, an effective academic setting will also foster other associations such as:

- Students' relationship with their peers
- Caregivers' relationships with their children
- School staff members' relationships with one another (p. 86)

Enrichment Mind-Set

The staff of an enrichment-type learning facility must also have an "enrichment mind-set." Students excel when they are in a nurturing environment that promotes excellence and guides its participants toward high achievement.

> An enriched learning environment offers challenging, complex curriculum and instruction, provides the lowest-performing students with the most highly qualified teachers, minimizes stressors, boosts participation in physical activity and the arts, ensures that students get good nutrition, and provides students with the support they need to reach high expectations. (Jensen, 2009, p. 94)

Conclusion

A significant characteristic of MLE is the importance of a mediator (adult) engaging the child and giving meaning to a stimulus. Enrichment programs must be conscience that their objective is to develop the cognitive function of students and not just expose them to alternative environments, as exposure alone does not generate change. "Repeated actions, unaccompanied by thinking and understanding processes, may perhaps cause enjoyment and reinforcement but do not necessarily produce learning" (Feuerstein, 2010, p. 32). Establishments that serve low-SES students understandably desire to give these children new opportunities and experiences, but before SCM transpires, deliberate, planned interaction between mediator and learner must take place.

Educational pedagogy and methodologies, brain studies, etc. will certainly appear overwhelming to the individual volunteering to tutor a child an hour a week at their local church. It is important to stress that an in-depth knowledge of these topics is not necessary to provide the type of mediational environment detailed by Professor Reuven Feuerstein. First, an understanding and acceptance of the biblical mandate given to Christians to support those in poverty is essential. Second, the religious or community program that endeavors to increase the academic performance of children, especially those in low-SES communities, must be open to the training of its staff and volunteers by outside professionals. Jensen's SHARE method, when combined with the impact of Feuerstein's Mediated Learning Experience, can create a rewarding learning experience for both teacher and student.

As Christians who educate families from impoverished homes and communities, the objective must not only be improving math and reading skills, but also to present the student with an environment contrary to the one he or she may be accustomed. After the environment has been introduced, modeled, and practiced over time, one will see a shift in thinking and behavior. Behavior that has been modified through MLE creates permanent change and builds cognitive skills that can be applied to future endeavors; as educators, the creation of Christian, independent thinkers with the faculty to reason and draw logical conclusions must be the goal for our students.

References

Exodus 23:11. (2017) Retrieved from https://www.godvine.com/bible/exodus/23-11.

Feuerstein, R., Falik, L. H., & Feuerstein, R. S. (2015). *Changing minds & brains.* New York, NY: Teachers College Press.

Feuerstein, R., Feuerstein, R. S., & Falik, L. H. (2010). Beyond smarter: *Mediated learning and the brains capacity for change.* New York, NY: Teachers College Press.

Feuerstein, R., Rand, Y., & Haywood, H. C. (1995). *Learning propensity assessment device manual.* Jerusalem, Israel: The International Center for the Enhancement of Learning Potential.

Feuerstein, R., Feuerstein, R. S., Rand, Y., & Falik, L. H. (2006). *Creating and enhancing cognitive modifiability: The Feuerstein Instrumental Enrichment program.* Jerusalem, Israel: ICELP Publications.

Fulgham, Nicole Baker. (2013). *Educating all God's Children.* Grand Rapids, MI: Brazos Press.

Hare, D. R. (1993). *Interpretation, A Bible commentary for teaching and preaching.* Louisville, KY: John Knox Press.

Jensen, E. (2005). *Teaching with the brain in mind.* Alexandria, VA: Association for Supervision and Curriculum Development (ASCD).

Jensen, E. (2009). *Teaching with poverty in mind.* Alexandria, VA: ASCD.

Jensen, E. (2013). *Engaging students with poverty in mind.* Alexandria, VA: ASCD.

Lynch, M. (2016). *The 20th Century and education's war on poverty.* Richmond, VA: The Edvocate.

Moreland, J. P. (1996) *Love your God with all your mind.* Colorado Springs, CO: NavPress

Payne, R. K. (2005). *A framework for understanding poverty.* Highlands, TX: aha! Process Inc.

Pfeiffer, C., & Harrison, E. F. (1962). *The Wycliffe Bible Commentary.* Chicago, IL: Moody Press.

Pfeiffer, C., & Harrison, E. F. (1990). *The Wycliffe Bible Commentary.* Chicago, IL: Moody Press.

Poverty Thresholds. (2016, September 1). Retrieved from U.S. Census Bureau: www.census.gov.

Poverty Tract. (2015, December 29). Retrieved from ArcGIS: https://www. arcgis.com.

Tan, O. S., & Seng, A. S. H. (2008). Cognitive modifiability and cognitive functions. In O. S. Tan, & A. S. H. Seng, *Cognitive modifiability in learning and assessment* (pp. 1-65). Singapore: Cengage Learning.

The Lockman Foundation. (1995). *New American Standard Bible.* La Habra, CA: Foundation Publications, Inc. .

Tribus, M. P., & Falik, L. L. (2001). *Mediating the development of character through mediated learning experience.* California.

Wilson, D., & Conyers, M. (2013). *Five big ideas for effective teaching.* New York: Teachers College Press.

Author Biography

Dena Moss Moten, Ed.D. has been an educator for 20 years with a focus on students living in low socioeconomic communities. She also teaches and trains women in the area of spiritual growth.

Walking Alongside Single Parents in the Church

Kevin Clark Jones

Karen walked into church on Sunday, toting three children and a diaper bag. She had hoped to get everyone to church in time for Sunday School before the worship service, but after several meltdowns over clothing choices and a breakfast mishap, it just was not possible. "We're here, though," she thought, "that's better than I can say for last week." The previous week, her ex-husband had the kids all day Saturday. When he was two hours late bringing them back, well past bedtime, she knew church was out of the question the next day. However, her family of four was in church that day, looking for a glimmer of hope. It had been nine months since Karen's husband left, and it had been difficult emotionally, financially, and spiritually.

"Please, Jesus, remind me that you're with us," she prayed as the pastor stepped to the pulpit to give the opening announcements. The worship songs that day lifted her soul, and she was thankful for the loving volunteers that taught her kids in children's church, so she could be present for the sermon. After church, several other church members asked how she was doing. "Fine," she would reply, "we are taking it day by day." These pleasantries, while well-intentioned, did little to ease her struggle. "I wish just someone would offer to watch my kids one night this week, even for just one hour," she thought, feeling guilty for her bitterness. As loving as her church family was on Sunday, she hardly heard from any of them the rest of the week. Church was no longer a place of joy, as it was before her husband left. It was now a reminder that, even among God's people, she was all alone.

Single mothers like Karen are likely attending every one of our churches. Many are barely treading the waters of financial stability but are too embarrassed to ask for help. Meanwhile, single fathers feel inadequate to raise their children but feel asking for help would show a weakness they are unwilling to share. James 1:27 commands God's people to care for the orphan and widow, echoing at least seven Old Testament passages reflecting the same sentiment (McKnight, 2011, p. 169).[1] Scholarly commentators contend this includes children and parents who have been effectively orphaned and widowed by divorce. Proceeding sections will show that churches must intentionally minister to single parents in relevant and practical ways.

In response to an identified need at a particular church, this researcher authored and taught a family discipleship course, which not only taught parents to disciple their children, but also presented a plan for the church to minister to the needs of single parents. The course included a pre-course and post-course survey to determine the participant's perceptions on how well the course answered the needs of single parents. Justification for classifying single parents and their children as widows and orphans and a scholarly justification for the applicability of the book of James to this topic will be introduced in the following paragraphs.

The Biblical Mandate

"Religion that is pure and undefiled before God, the Father, is this: to visit orphans and widows in their affliction" (James 1:27a, ESV). The Old Testament declares God as the "Father of the fatherless and protector of widows" (Psalm 68:5, ESV). The word for "orphan" has also been shown to refer to children who have lost only one parent, thus translated "fatherless" or "motherless" (McKnight, 2011, p. 170). Whatever the case may be, the orphan and widow "become types of those who find themselves helpless in the world" (Moo, 2000, p. 86). Single parents and their children have effectively been orphaned and widowed and should be considered among those who find themselves helpless.

In the context of James 1, verses 26 and 27 serve as a summary statement for the ethical position of James' letter, emphasizing the requirement for Christians to be "doers" of their faith (McKnight, 2011, p. 162). James 1:22 urges readers not to deceive themselves by reading the Word and ignoring it; verses 26 and 27 give specific examples of what this looks like (McKnight, 2011, p. 162). Verse 26 specifically offers a sobering reminder that religious practices can be honorable, but an ethical, compassionate heart must accompany them, or religion is useless and self-deceptive (Davids, 1989, p. 42). As McCartney (2011) notes, James' condemnation of false religion echoes that of the prophet Jeremiah in verses such as this: "every goldsmith is put to shame by his idols, for his images are false, and there is no breath in them. They are worthless, a work of delusion; at the time of their punishment they shall perish (Jeremiah 51:17b-18, ESV).

Continuing in James 1:27, the phrase "to visit" implies oversight, caring, and assistance rather than simple visitation (MacArthur, 1998, p. 89). Often, this word is used regarding the visitation of God to save His people, such as in Acts 20:28 where a variation of this word is translated as "overseer" (MacArthur, 1998, p. 89).[2] Genesis 50:24 provides an example of God's saving visitation, saying: "And Joseph said to his brothers, 'I am about to die, but God will visit you and bring you up out of this land to the land that he swore to Abraham, to Isaac, and to Jacob'" (Genesis 50:24, ESV, Emphasis mine). Here, "visit" is the translation of the Hebrew word paqad (Johnson, 1995, p. 212). Thus, used in James 1:27, the phrase highlights the covenantal obligation people have to care for others and "oversee" the needs of the afflicted (Johnson, 1995, p. 212). Even if these family members are afflicted due to their own sin, the church can assist and "visit" them without endorsing their sin, valuing the people formed in God's image, and pointing them toward the healing gospel (Remy, 2015, p. 93).

The orphan and widow were included among the "traditional poor" in early Israel, along with foreigners and Levites (Davids, 1989, p. 43). Douglas Moo (2000) reflects on the utter helplessness of orphans and widows and extends affliction to others who are helpless, saying:

> Christians whose religion is pure will imitate their Father by intervening to help the helpless. Those who suffer from want in the third world, in the inner city; those who are unemployed and penniless; those who are inadequately represented in government or

in law – these are the people who should see abundant evidence of
Christians' pure religion. (p. 86)

The ultimate truth Christians learn from this passage is that truly following Jesus means serving those who are hurting and in need. Single parents and their children, especially single mothers, are among the neediest
people in our churches.[3] We must address these needs and serve them as
God commanded through James. A whole section of the Family Ministry
course is devoted to this command.

Findings

This family ministry course was taught to both traditional parents and
single parents. Six traditional families and four single parents took both the
pre-course and post-course survey. As James 1:27 and single-parent ministry were presented, many traditional families expressed concern for the
needs of the single parents sitting right next to them. In general, however,
survey results showed that the course did very little to ease their struggle.

In order to identify whether or not the course led to a statistically significant difference, a ¬t-test for dependent samples was administered to
the pre-course survey and post-course survey. This survey, which asked
questions regarding the stability of family situations, was taken by both
traditional families and single parents. For this article, only results from
single parents will be discussed. Among single parents, only one area did
the survey reflect any form of improvement, and it was clear that a simple
six-week course was not all that single parents needed.

Below are the most significant results of the pre- and post-survey given
to single parents. Each following item represents a need this course wished
to address.

1. Single parents were asked if they felt guilt regarding their marital
   decisions and how they affected their children. There was no significant improvement ($t(3) = 1$, p $= .391$), showing that the course did
   not decrease guilt felt about marital decisions.
2. Parents were asked if someone else's decisions had negatively affected their children. Results indicated that this course did not reduce

the feeling that someone else's decisions had negatively affected their children ($t(3) = 0, p = 1$).

3. Parents were asked if they felt adequately equipped to navigate difficult family situations. There was no significant improvement ($t(3) = .225, p = .836$), showing that the course was inadequate in helping parents with difficult family situations.

4. Parents were asked if they believed their children had mentors other than their parents. There was a statistically significant improvement ($t(3) = 4.333, p = .023$), indicating that single parents felt an increase of Godly mentors for their children throughout the course.[4]

5. Parents were asked if the church adequately addressed the needs of their families. Results indicated that, in general, parents believed the church did a fair job of addressing the needs of their families. However, the lack of improvement in this area showed that the course was not enough to help single parents ($t(3) = .293, p = .789$).

6. Parents were asked if they felt isolated from other families in the church. Results showed that there was no significant improvement in feelings of isolation among the participants ($t(3) = 1.127, p = .342$).

So, what can be done? If a simple course is not enough, what should the church do? Findings from this research show that churches must establish a consistent, on-going, intentional ministry to single parents. The church must mentor children of single parents, especially men of the church mentoring the male children of single mothers. While this research admitted possible weaknesses in both the research instrument and the sample size, these findings show that the church must find appropriate ways to provide for the practical needs of single parents.

Single Parents and the Church

To bypass the orphan in favor of a focus on whole and healthy families is to neglect a heartbeat that has long marked the rhythms of God's redemptive plan...There are, after all, no natural-born children of God among us; there are only ex-orphans who have been brought into God's family through divine adoption (Jones, 2011, p. 191).

As stated above, the widow and the orphan are of special interest to God and thus to the people of God. God commanded His people to care for the fatherless seven times in the giving of the Law (Jones, 2011, p. 168).[5] The simple and profound truth of the gospel compels Christian families around the orphan and widow to become family to them (Jones, 2011, p. 168). Churches must focus not on the "earthly heritage" of brokenness that especially effects single parents and their children, but on divine adoption into sonship and daughtership in the kingdom of God (Jones, 2011, p. 169).

Harley Atkinson (1997) states that "the quality or lack of quality in family life today is a key contributor to the critical condition of our current youth generation" (p. 15). She cites empirical studies showing that between forty and sixty percent of children will live with only one parent for some amount of time before reaching the age of eighteen (Atkinson, 1997, p. 15). Because of this, single parents must navigate their children's feelings of abandonment and portray God as a loving father when even the idea of a loving father may be a concept entirely foreign to them. Les Parrott notes, "The emotional trauma and pain of losing your parents through the dissolution of their marriage is, without question, one of the most significant factors contributing to the struggles teens cope with in the aftermath of parental divorce" (Parrott, 2000, p. 293).

In divorce, children lose the completeness of their family and experience loss of relationships with both parents due to the changing family structure (Granot, 2005, p. 123). The loss of familiarity in relationships often effects children long term and must be grieved and worked through with care (Granot, 2005, p. 124). This is accentuated when a parent leaves and either breaks all ties with the children or detaches emotionally from them (Granot, 2005, p. 127-128). Some studies have shown that, even if a parent initially attempts to remain in contact with the children, the contact he or she maintains decreases two years after the divorce (Hetherinton, Cox & Cox, 1982, p. 251).

Without support from the church, children are often left without answers to the difficult questions these circumstances initiate, and parents need to be equipped to help their children through it. Parents face the difficult challenge of attempting to help their children face divorce while they themselves are experiencing the same or more intense negative emotions. Single parents are often suddenly on their own and face fear involving how to parent alone, how to cope with loss, how to manage finances, and how to trust God in the midst of tragedy (Miller, 1994, pp. 212-213). Doubt and uncertainty flood the minds of parents right after divorce as coping with new family situations becomes a reality (Miller, 1994, p. 228). Single mothers may face economic issues that affect decisions about work and childcare, as well as issues of time (Miller, 1994, p. 218). Single fathers may feel inadequate to sustain new parental roles (Miller, 1994, p. 216). Both, especially single mothers, may "have no other adult to turn to for help" (Miller, 1994, p. 218). The church can provide single parents with help in these areas, supporting them simply by being available!

Children and adolescents who experience parental divorce "mourn the death of that marriage, just as they would mourn the death of a parent" (Parrott, 2000, p. 294). Parents can help their children through this by walking them through the stages of grief (denial, anger, bargaining, depression, and acceptance) and the church can equip them to do so (Parrott, 2000, p. 294). Parents must understand that the rhythms of grief experienced by their children will be much different than their own; while adults (and some adolescents) dwell on grief for months or even years, some children and adolescents dwell on grief for shorter periods and may seem to block out the traumatic event at times (Granot, 2005, p. 150). Reflecting on this, Tamar Granot (2005) says this:

> Just as much as the child needs the support and encouragement of the adult to express his distress, he also needs him as a model at the stage of emotional acceptance and adjustment. The child needs the example of the coping parent. He needs to get the message that it is okay to resume life. He draws strength from the 'permission' given by his parent to go on with his life. (p. 150)

The reduction of fear in a child's life depends on his or her parent's reaction to anxiety caused by divorce; single parents must aim to assuage fear (Granot, 2005, pp. 156-157).

Children of divorce will likely distrust all adults after parental separation, wondering who they can rely on (Van Pelt & Hancock, 2005, p. 146). This is where the church must step in. Church leaders must be present in the lives of children of divorce, giving them reliable adults in which to confide (Van Pelt & Hancock, 2005, p. 147). A reliable friend and mentor in the church can provide much needed stability for the child (Clinton, 2010, p. 209). As churches consider single-parent ministry, they must create an environment that encourages others to mentor children of single parents. Occasionally, children of single mothers' lack positive father figures in their lives; in the absence of such, male leadership in the church must strive to mentor those children.

For parents, especially the parent remaining in the life of the child, rebuilding trust means making children the priority, taking time to talk with him or her about "life, hopes, struggles, ambitions, and relationships" (Clinton, 2010, p. 209). When engaging single-parent ministry, churches must encourage parents to be open and honest with their children regarding plans involving living arrangements and other aspects of life after divorce (Rowatt, 1989, p. 87). Helping single parents communicate successfully with their children can help begin to repair broken relationships (Ehrlich, 2014, p. 139).

Conclusion

Even in a gospel-centered church, single parents can be inadvertently overlooked. Churches must intentionally minister to them and "yearn to see the gospel bring new life to broken people" (Remy, 2015, p. 91). This research found that a six-week family discipleship course drew attention to some the needs of single parents, particularly to mentor their children, but was not adequate to meet all of their needs. A church that desires to help single parents must continually and intentionally minister to, support, and care for them.

References

Clinton, Timothy E. (2010). *The Quick-Reference Guide to Counseling Teenagers.* Grand Rapids, MI: Baker Books.

Davids, Peter H. (1989). *James*. Peabody, MA: Hendrickson Publishers.

Ehrlich, Joshua. (2014). *Divorce and Loss: Helping Adults and Children Mourn When a Marriage Comes Apart*. Lanham, MD: Rowman & Littlefield.

Granot, Tamar. (2005). *Without You: Children and Young People Growing Up With Loss and Its Effects*. London; Philadelphia, PA: Jessica Kingsley Publishers.

Hetherinton, E. Mavis, Cox, Martha, & Cox, Roger. (1982). "Effects of Divorce on Parents and Children." In *Nontraditional Families: Parenting and Child Development*, edited by Michael E. Lamb. Hillsdale, NJ: L. Erlbaum Associates.

Johnson, Luke Timothy. (1995). *The Letter of James: A New Translation With Introduction and Commentary*. New York, NY: Doubleday.

Jones, Timothy P. (2011). *Family Ministry Field Guide: How Your Church Can Equip Parents to Make Disciples*. Indianapolis, IN: Wesleyan Publishing House.

MacArthur, John. (1998). *James*. The MacArthur New Testament Commentary. Chicago, IL: Moody Press.

McCartney, Dan. (2009). *James*. Baker Exegetical Commentary on the New Testament. Grand Rapids, MI: Baker Academic.

McKnight, Scot. (2011). *The Letter of James*. The New International Commentary on the New Testament. Grand Rapids, MI: W.B. Eerdmans Publishing Company.

Miller, David R. (1994). *Counseling Families After Divorce*. Contemporary Christian Counseling 8. Dallas, TX: Word.

Moo, Douglas J. (2000). *The Letter of James*. Grand Rapids, MI; Leicester, England: William B. Eerdmans; Apollos.

Parrott, Les. (2000). *Helping the Struggling Adolescent: A Guide to Thirty-Six Common Problems for Counselors, Pastors, and Youth Workers*. Updated and expanded. Grand Rapids, MI: Zondervan Publishing House.

Remy, Joshua A. (2015). "Be a Family for Blended Families." In *Practical Family Ministry*, edited by Timothy P. Jones and John David Trentham, 89–98. Nashville, TN: Randall House.

Rowatt, Wade. (1989). *Pastoral Care with Adolescents in Crisis*. 1st ed. Louisville, KY: Westminster/J. Knox Press.

Van Pelt, Rich, & Hancock, Jim. (2005). *The Youth Worker's Guide to Helping Teenagers in Crisis*. Grand Rapids, MI: Zondervan.

Wolfinger, Nicholas. (2015, January 8). "The Changing Economics of Single Motherhood." *Pacific Standard*. Retrieved from https://psmag.com/economics/changing-economics-single-motherhood-97360.

Endnotes

[1] See: Exodus 22:22; Deuteronomy 10:18, 24:17, 27:19; Psalm 10:14, 146:9; Isaiah 1:23.

[2] Acts 20:28, ESV. See also: 1 Timothy 3:2 and Titus 1:7 for Paul's usage of this root word.

[3] In 2013, single mothers were five times more likely to be in poverty than traditional families (Wolfinger, 2015).

[4] As a result of the course, a men's camping trip was planned with the intentional purpose of mentoring and building relationships with the male children of the single parents in the course.

[5] See: Exodus 22:22-24; Deuteronomy 10:18, 14:29, 16:11-14, 24:17-21, 26:12-13, 27:19.

Author Biography

Kevin Clark Jones is the Family Pastor at Fox Hill Road Baptist Church in Hampton, Virginia. He received his D.Ed.Min. in Family Ministry from Southern Baptist Theological Seminary in December 2017.

Practioner Insights

The D6 Family Journal editorial board helped design the uniqueness of this journal. This section entitled Practitioner Reflections offers you a look at family ministry from practitioners engaged in preschool, children, student, college, adults, or senior ministry. The practitioner reflections do not submit to the same academic peer review process but still pass through multiple editors before becoming part of the volume. We believe this section will allow insightful ministry leaders the chance to present an area facing the church today.

Your Children's Children: The Impact of Grandparents and Extended Family on Children's Spiritual Development

Dr. Susan Willhauck

Abstract: This essay explores biblical and modern considerations in the experience of grandparents or other extended family members who take their grandchildren to church and/or provide them with spiritual guidance. It will delve into the role of proxy faith mentors, the importance of faith formation across generations and then identify some implications and practical suggestions for ministry.

I teach at a small seminary and I have noticed that as the younger students share their faith histories, an increasing number of them say their grandparents were their primary faith mentors or had the most influence on their spiritual development, perhaps even their decision to follow a call to ministry. From speaking with faculty at other seminaries, my sense is that this is fairly common. We live in a "graying society" and one is likely to see more older persons in our congregations than persons 20-50 years of age (Census data 2000 and 2010; Pew Resource Center, 2010). These older people, however, may have a distinctive opportunity to minister with the youngest generations that we should not overlook.

The key role of grandparents and extended family in the raising of children is not a new idea. The *paideia* of children has historic roots in early Jewish and Christian communities. The Bible contains many references to adult obligations to teach, discipline, and care for children. Patrick D. Miller writes of the communal and cross-generational responsibility for the moral education of children that the book of Deuteronomy addresses (Miller, 2008). Biblical scholar Margaret Y. MacDonald's (2014) interesting book, *The Power of Children: The Construction of Christian Families in the Greco-Roman World*, discusses patterns of kinship and household codes in the Pastoral Epistles that attest to grandmothers' (in particular) roles in the socialization of children in the faith.

The phenomenon of grandparents nurturing the faith of the next generation has not escaped the notice of recent researchers. *Families and Faith: How Religion is Passed Down Across Generations*, the work of noted gerontologist Vern L. Bengtson, et al., is a sociological study which examined intergenerational religious perpetuity and discovered an "unexpected importance of grandparents and great-grandparents" (Bengtson, Putney & Harris, 2013). Their data revealed that recent generations will have greater involvement with their grandparents than any previous generation in American history because of an increase in life expectancy. Since grandchildren have living grandparents for longer, this has increased the chances for grandparents having a larger role in the child's life. Although there is sometimes more geographic distance between them than in the past, there is also more technology to support communication such as Facebook, Skype, and Face-time. There are other reasons for grandparents taking on a proxy role as faith mentors, according to Bengtson, et al., such as a growing number of single-parent households, a larger number of grandparents providing direct care for grandchildren than ever before, and increasing numbers of grandparents who are raising grandchildren full-time because their own adult children are unable to parent (Bengtson, Putney & Harris, 2013). In 2010, 4.9 million children under the age of 18 lived in grandparent headed households, which was up from 4.5 million ten years prior (AARP, 2010).

Another qualitative research study in 2014 interviewed grandparents who take their children to church regularly. These grandparents indicated that their adult children lacked interest in church, but even though they were not motivated to attend worship themselves, did not object to their parents taking their children on Sunday mornings. In some cases, it is the grandchild who initiates the church-going. One of the study participants recalled how her four-year-old granddaughter told her mother, "I want to go to church with grandpa and grandma. Please ask them to take me" (Otto, 2014).

Bengtson, et.al. identified four types of religious influence of grand-parents:

- The "skipped generation," influence. This is grandparents substituting for parents as proxy faith mentors, as in the Otto research.
- Grandparents reinforcing or enhancing parental religious influence.
- Grandparents challenging or subverting the lack of parental religious socialization against the wishes of their adult children.
- Grandparents who ignore or abdicate any role in the faith formation of their grandchildren.

In general, Bengtson, et al. found more religious continuity between grandparents and grandchildren than between parents and children. Culture also plays a part in the degree of influence. African American families, for example, place a significant emphasis on the wisdom and influence of elders and extended families in the teaching of the faith to the young. The family collective that is the norm in some parts of the world is becoming increasingly present in North America (Wimberly & Parker, 2003).

Grandparents also report that they benefit spiritually from their grandchildren. Taking their grandchildren to church gives them a kind of renewed purpose. Bengtson et al. compares this to the experience of generativity in Erikson's theory of the life cycle. There is a kind of reverse socialization in which the younger generation also instructs the older (Bengtson, Putney & Harris, 2013). In the grandparent-grandchild relationship, there is the possibility for listening and connection that busy and stressed parents sometimes neglect. This is a spiritual connection that can be transforming for both grandparent and grandchild.

In the 18th and 19th centuries John Wesley, Schleiermacher, and Bushnell argued that parents and the Christian home are the primary teachers of the faith (Bunge, 2001). While congregations and programs do not replace this function, they can offer another support for the passing on of faith to children. Recognizing and celebrating the role of grandparents in faith formation does not diminish the need and mandate for parental responsibility in the faith development of their children. It is to simply acknowledge that today's families may look differently than they did a generation or two ago, and that grandparents may provide (in the absence of parental influence) or enhance the parental role. More theological reflection is called for on the vocation of parenting and grandparenting and on the potential of the extended family in our changing cultures for bringing up children in the Christian faith. Here are some ideas that clergy, lay leaders, and Christian educators might consider:

- Be understanding of the challenges that families face today and recognize that families may struggle in less than ideal relationships. Be welcoming and supportive of grandparents (and other relatives) who bring their grandchildren to church for whatever reason. Acknowledge their story and challenges without singling them out unnecessarily. Leaders' attitudes are crucial. Instead of dwelling on the negative (the missing generations), see the positive potential in grandparents serving God in this way.

- Preach and teach that you welcome intergenerational families, so when you talk about family ministry, family nights, or activities, it is clear that all are welcome.

- Provide resources and suggestions to grandparents for talking with their grandchildren about Christianity and faith and for practicing Christian virtues. Theologically speaking, grandparenting can be viewed as a call to witness the love of Jesus to the younger generation. It has been called "a sacred gift" to be a faith mentor and friend in this way. Several books explore grandparenting from a Christian perspective and may be shared with grandparents in our congregations (Huntly, 2001; Milton & Milton, 2007; Small & Small, 2016).

- Include prayers for grandparents in worship and in your devotions. Or have intergenerational families lead in worship by reading Scripture or leading prayers.

- Consider starting a grandparents' group for prayer, study, and fellowship. Invite speakers who can address specific topics helpful to them.

- Grandparents who experience resistance from their adult children in exerting too much influence may need particular pastoral care. Perhaps they want to have more opportunity to help their grandchildren's spiritual development but may be afraid of interfering too much. When grandparents do not share the religious tradition or beliefs of the parents, there can be particular concern. Still there can be a meaningful spiritual connection. Talk with them about how they can navigate the relationship with their adult children and help them find ways to open or re-visit the conversation.

- Help grandparents to understand that even if they do not have direct input into their grandchildren's faith formation, they can be a vital witness by living the Christian life and praying for their grandchildren.

- Encourage all congregants to take an active role in the spiritual development of the children in the congregation as is promised in baptismal covenants. This includes sharing one's faith, speaking to and getting to know the children, possibly teaching Sunday School. Again, preach and teach on the communal and intergenerational responsibility for the transmission of the faith. The congregation may be one of the few remaining places where intergenerational connections are fostered.

- Because some children do not have grandparents who have religious influence in their lives, and because some older adults do not have grandchildren, churches could have an "adopt a grandkid" program in which older adults are assigned to a child in the church to give special attention (sit with in worship, send cards, share stories).
- Recognize that consistency is important for children whose lives are otherwise inconsistent. Extended family and grandparents and leaders in a congregation can offer that crucial consistency with their time and presence.
- Have an intergenerational gift-sharing event. Invite both older and younger people to share a skill or craft or music from their generation. Examples might include a cooking lesson, teaching dance steps, or how to use an iphone.
- Moderate a panel discussion for older and younger generations to discuss current events in the news and how families can be a guiding force in a turbulent world.

Christians acknowledge and confess human failing in our world. Sin and its consequences follows us from generation to generation. Families and relationships sometimes reflect that brokenness. But in keeping with the biblical mandate, we also proclaim the good news of God's grace across those generations with our children and our children's children. Many of today's grandparents know that children are a vital part of the Christian church and are promised the blessings that reverence and love of the Lord brings. Let us lift up the faith inspiring grandparents in our midst!

References

American Association of Retired Persons (2010). http://www.aarp.org/relationships/grandparenting/info-12-2010/more_grandparents_raising_grandchildren.html.

Bengtson, V. L., Putney, N. M., & Harris, S. (2013). *Families and faith: How religion is passed down across generations*. New York, NY: Oxford University Press.

Bunge, M. J. (2001). *The child in Christian thought*. Grand Rapids, MI: William B. Eerdmans Publishing Company.

Census Data (2000 and 2010). https://www.census.gov/prod/2014pubs/p25-1140.pdf.

Huntly, A. (2001). *The sacred gift of grandparenting*. Etobicoke, ON: United Church of Canada.

MacDonald, M. Y. (2014). *The power of children: The construction of Christian families in the Greco-Roman world*. Waco, TX: Baylor University Press.

Miller, P. D. (2008). That the children may know: Children in Deuteronomy. In M. J. Bunge (Ed.), *The child in the Bible* (pp. 45-62). Grand Rapids: MI: William B. Eerdmans Publishing Company.

Milton R. & Milton B. (2007). *The spirituality of grandparenting*. Kelowna, BC, Canada: Wood Lake Publishing.

Otto, L. G. (2014). *One generation away from extinction: Grandparents as primary religious educators of their grandchildren* (Master's thesis). Atlantic School of Theology.

Pew Research Center (2010). http://www.pewforum.org/2010/02/17/religion-among-the-millennials/.

Small, R. & Small, D. (2016). *Grandparenting: Creating and keeping a lasting legacy*. Spring City, PA: Morning Joy Media.

Wimberly, A. E. S., & Parker, E. L. (2003). *In Search of wisdom: Faith formation in the Black church*. Nashville, TN: Abingdon Press.

Author Biography

Dr. Susan Willhauck is an Associate Professor of Pastoral Theology at Atlantic School of Theology in Halifax, Nova Scotia. She also taught Christian Formation at Wesley Theological Seminary in Washington DC. She is co-author of *Qualitative Research in Theological Education: Pedagogy in Practice* (SCM Press, 2018).

Fatherless

Dr. Jody Dean

Psalm 68:5-6 "A father of the fatherless and a judge for the widows, Is God in His holy habitation. God makes a home for the lonely…" (NASB).

What does it mean?

The weight of the word "fatherless" just captures the mind to weigh the depths of being without a father in society where the father is a major aspect of your natural development. "The father is responsible for the overall development of the child."[1]

What is my heritage from my father? Fatherless to the extent no Father's Day cards are created as a child, no birthday or Christmas gifts made or purchased, no advice about dating, no college or career advice in high school, and that key male figure God intended to help shape a child into a person that follows after God is not there. The father's exhortation is highlighted in Scripture as a common occurrence. "We were exhorting and encouraging and imploring each one of you as a father would his own child" (1 Thess. 2:11, NASB). Paul is demonstrating the strength of a father's love by encouraging, comforting, and urging these people toward godly living.[2] The fatherless child does have the Christian father option to encourage their spiritual formation. A void that has to be filled from the mother but also Christian men that can mentor the child.

The Facts

As we begin to unpack the layers throughout childhood into a young adulthood a few terms need to be outlined for our discussion. Fatherless does not also mean a child is an orphan. Although a fatherless child could be motherless and totally alone and thus be orphaned, the following pages describe the single-parent home and the implications for the child and ministry. Each chapter will present a life stage, example, and reflections for ministry. Although one can be fatherless from birth, many have the experiences as a preschooler, child, or adolescent of having known their father and then being confronted with him no longer in their life. Webster's dictionary simply defines fatherless as someone not having a father living, lacking a father's protection, or not knowing the identity of one's father. A catastrophic crisis for a family to resolve is the loss of a member. The first Christmas or birthday cause the family to alter and even reconstruct traditions and rituals.[3] In my family, these served as vivid reminders that dad was not there. One grapples for memories or even strives not to forget the family member possibly through a favorite picture or treasure that one remembers dad loved. I know I have a collection of artifacts from dad that are cherished the more I mature in adulthood. Mom had to adjust to realize that friends that were couples now distanced themselves as they grieved and faded into the distance because a widow did not fit into the mix. A family even goes through a restructuring as the missing roles performed by dad have to be filled going forward. One may feel fatherless as a dad wrestles with a terminal illness and is no longer physically able to be a part of your life. Many adults deal with this transition as their parent ages and faces end of life sickness from Alzheimer's disease or stroke.[4]

The reality for children is that almost 1 out of 4 children live in a single-parent home with their mother.[5] The National Center for Fathering sums up the fatherless epidemic with the following quick facts[6]:

- 20 million children in the U. S. live in a fatherless home
- 4x more likely to be raised in poverty
- 90% of all homeless and runaway children are fatherless
- 71% of all adolescent substance abusers come from a fatherless home
- 10x more likely to abuse chemical substances
- 80% of adolescents in psychiatric hospitals come from fatherless homes
- 2x more likely to commit suicide
- 9x more likely to drop out of school
- Less likely to attain academic and professional qualifications in adulthood
- 70% of adolescents in juvenile correctional facilities come from fatherless homes
- 60% of rapists come from fatherless homes
- 11x more likely to have violent behavior

- 20x more likely to be incarcerated
- 70% of teen pregnancies happen in fatherless homes

The sources for these statistics are numerous but the bigger picture they reveal is that the faith community can help provide a solution. In the church, we are designed by God like a family. According to James Dobson the "chief among our concerns is the absence of a masculine role modeling and mentoring that dads should be providing."[7]

The Difference

In my life, I have been able to overcome fatherlessness due to a multitude of godly men who were willing to stand in the gap for me and be a role model and mentor. The statistics are stacked against those that find themselves fatherless as a minor but as people of faith we have a great opportunity to help these children overcome. I am a Ph.D. graduate, married, two children, not addicted, not been arrested, and have beat the statistics. I believe the godly men in my life as well as a godly widowed mother made the difference. James 1:27 reveals the importance of taking care of the widow and orphan while also taking care of our own walk with Christ.

James 1:23-25 exposes the concept of the mirror in our lives spiritually. He leads the reader to consider personal action as a result of hearing and responding to God's Word. In the middle of the verses a common everyday item is mentioned to cause the reader to pause and observe their lifestyle through the reflection of a mirror. In today's world, it would be the equivalent of scrolling a social media news feed with little memory about the actual people represented by the posts. You may be like me and have little memory of people beyond the punchline, pictures, and activities they share. The mirror James references in the passage represents the quick glance of looking at yourself to comb your hair or shave and quickly leaving that image and going about your day.

The deeper meaning for me as I reflect on this passage reveals the spiritual side of a mirror. Some days each of us only take the time for a quick glance for Bible reading or a brief prayer over a meal that only directs us toward God. If we live each day with just quick glimpses of God, then do we ever arrive at the place in our lives that will produce a lifestyle of ministry to the forgotten peoples of society?

A widow or an orphan represented a person that was totally dependent on others and for each of us to be a doer of the Word and not just a quick-glance hearer of the Word would minister to people. Jesus summarized this level of commitment as loving your neighbor. The evidence of a person that was living more in the Word than with quick glances toward God would not forget the least of these. "To visit orphans and widows means to seek them out with a deep concern for their well-being and a clear commitment to care for their needs."[8]

As the son of a widow, I believe that helping someone with a quick response that is easily forgotten does not change their plight or forecast in life to a great degree but makes the other person feel pretty good about themselves. This is not the level of ministry James is calling us toward. James is trying to help you and I understand that we need a deep devotion to the Word of God that leads to a lifestyle of committed response. If you and I can grasp that level of worth to the least of these, then our lives will touch everyone for a kingdom impact. Will each of us begin to look deeply into the mirror and forget the quick glance approach of simply being presentable in public but unworthy to be presented to the feet of Jesus?

Each stage in our development presents a crisis to resolve. Both parents are crucial at navigating their children through these and when one is missing the challenge for the parent and child are even harder. "The blessing is a way of helping children and even adults experience at the deepest level of their hearts the certainty that they are highly valued and forever treasured by someone incredibly significant in their life stories."[9] The hurt a child can face due to being fatherless can create a huge void in their life. The concept of blessing can be filled from the mother or even a significant adult in the child's life. "Children simply don't have the maturity or understanding to deal with hurt and pain, so they tend to grab on to anything they can find to protect themselves and help them cope. Whatever works—athletic prowess, academic success, good looks, even drugs or alcohol—they want to repeat. By the time they grow up, they may have created layer upon layer of self-protection."[10]

The Old Testament provides a vivid picture of the desire a child has to receive a blessing from his father. Esau pleaded with his dad to bless him as well. A sad picture of a mother's jealousy and choosing one child over another. Many children feel like Esau for a myriad of reasons.

Endnotes

[1]Leroy Eims, The Lost Art of Disciple Making, (Grand Rapids, MI: Zondervan, 1978), 66.

[2]Max Anders, editor. Holman New Testament Commentary vol. 9, (Nashville,TN: Broadman and Holman, 2000), 25.

[3]Diana R. Garland, Family Ministry, (Downers Grove, IL: InterVarsity Press, 1999), 588.

[4]Ibid., 589.

[5]A Child's Day: Living Arrangements, Nativity, and Family Transitions: 2011 (Selected Indicators of Child Well-Being Issued December 2014. https://www.census .gov/content/dam/Census/library/publications/2014/demo/p70-139.pdf.

[6]Fatherless Epidemic. Fathers.com/wp39/wp-content/uploads/2015/05/fatherlessInfographic.png.

[7]James Dobson, Bringing Up Boys, (Carol Stream, IL: Tyndale Momentum, 2001), 55.

[8]David Platt, Counter Culture, (Carol Stream, IL: Tyndale House, 2015), 82.

[9]John Trent and Gary Smalley, The Blessing: Revised and Updated, (Nashville, TN: Thomas Nelson, 2011), 6.

[10]Ibid., 10.

Author Biography

Jody Dean, Ph.D. leads the extension center program at New Orleans Baptist Theological Seminary. He has a book being released Spring 2018 entitled: *Together We Equip: Integrating Discipleship and Ministry Leadership for Holistic Spiritual Formation.*

Book Reviews

    The book reviews submitted offer a critique of some of the latest family ministry titles. If you would like to see a title reviewed in the future, please submit at least two copies of either the book or galley copy (Publisher's PDF proof is acceptable if not yet published or to galley stage).

Linhart, Terry. *The Self-Aware Leader: Discovering Your Blind Spots to Reach Your Ministry Potential.* Downers Grove, IL: IVP, 2017. 184 pages. $16.00. Paper.

Review by John Fix, COO of Urban Youth Impact

Every teenager with a new permit is taught early and often of the dangers of not checking their blind spots when driving. Motorists can be extremely careful in all other elements of driver safety, but if they ignore these blind spots there is the potential for accidents and great harm to happen. And the perils are not just limited to the person behind the wheel. Failure to keep an eye on these areas can cause pain and suffering to countless others on the road. In his book *The Self-Aware Leader*, author Terry Linhart uses this same automobile analogy to demonstrate the importance for all Christian leaders to take time to assess their own hidden shortcomings. Failure to do so can not only crash your organization's mission, but it can also cause emotional damage to both the leader and the people they lead.

Linhart begins each chapter by explaining key areas of our lives where these pitfalls to effectiveness can hide. By using stories from his own personal growth journey as a leader, he helps the reader to shine light on areas of past hurt, temptations, slowly growing pressures, and personal boundary issues that can stunt our ability to direct and develop the people that God has put in our charge.

The Self-Aware Leader is not your typical leadership book that lists the ten things you can do to instantly be more effective in directing your team. It is not a book you can read though in one sitting and glean a few invaluable nuggets to transform you into a Fortune 500 CEO. Rather, it is a book that you must work through purposefully, one chapter at a time. Terry provides "self-check" questions after explaining each potential blind spot that requires time and brutal honesty to work through.

I found, however, that when I was willing to take the time to stare in the mirror, acknowledge my weaknesses, and truly put in an effort to work on them, that the potential for growth was far more valuable for me than just reading about someone else's tips that got them to the top.

The Self-Aware Leader is not a quick read, but it isn't meant to be. It is a book for people who understand that being good at anything takes a lot of work and practice. Linhart has provided an invaluable workbook that can be used as a periodic checkup to ensure you are succeeding in the areas that provide the greatest potential for failure. If you are looking for a book that challenges you to see yourself as you really are, helps you identify blind spots in your leadership, and helps you wrestle through these issues until you can improve them, then you will love the guidance that Linhart provides in these pages.

Talbot, Christopher. *Remodeling Youth Ministry: A Biblical Blueprint for Ministering to Students*. Gallatin, TN: Welch College Press, 2017. 195 pages. $17.99. Paper.

Review by Christopher Sanchez, Education and Evangelism Pastor at Northside Baptist Church in Valdosta, Georgia.

In *Remodeling Youth Ministry: A Biblical Blueprint for Ministering to Students*, Talbot sets the goal of inspiring the youth and family minister to think more deeply about his ministry and the souls he ministers to. He separates the book into three parts: (1) Laying the Foundation, (2) Making Renovations, and (3) Building for the Future. In part one, Talbot addresses the question "Is Youth Ministry Biblical?" He draws the attention of the reader to the tension that exists in answering this important question first with a "no" in that youth ministry should not be segregated from the church. He then answers the question with a "yes" concluding youth ministry is biblical when it occurs in the home and the church. The next two chapters clarify the purpose of youth ministry and the future of youth ministry and the church.

Four chapters form Making Renovations, part two of the book. Here Talbot offers his thoughts on specific remodeling tasks necessary in youth ministry. Chapter four gets right to the heart of the matter: making the gospel the focal point and not only teaching youth to share their faith, but to live out their faith as well. In chapter five Talbot rightly points out that what youth and family ministers teach and demonstrate as being important shape students in very powerful ways. He then addresses the means and methodology connecting preaching, fellowship, prayer, and service specifically to youth ministry.

Talbot devotes an entire chapter to rethinking apologetics. He argues one of the purposes of apologetics in youth ministry is to help students develop confidence in and develop the ability to defend their faith. The development of a Christian worldview is a right and proper goal of youth ministry. Rather than focusing on an evidential approach to apologetics,

Talbot argues for a presuppositional approach as better helping to develop a holistic understanding of their own faith and the world around them. He acknowledges there are challenges youth and family ministers will face shifting from teaching evidential apologetics to presuppositional apologetics making a strong case for the later. Part two concludes in chapter seven with Talbot arguing for a family as church/church as family ministry paradigm.

In part three, also four chapters, Talbot looks to the future. He writes of the foundation that must be in place before changes can be made in chapter eight. The primacy of Scripture in youth ministry is emphasized while also stressing the importance of coupling it with methodology. Talbot argues for organic change in which leadership sustainability is comprised of character and consistency on the part of young ministers that also allows for the slow pace of positive change in ministry. A timely reminder that all pastors, including youth pastors, have as their primary responsibility teaching and preaching the Word of God. Talbot addresses teaching teens particularly in chapter nine and the specific challenges technology presents in youth and family ministry in chapter ten. The concluding chapter urges those who serve in youth and family ministry to make rest one of their priorities.

Talbot accomplishes his goal of inspiring the youth and family minister to think more deeply about his ministry and the souls he ministers to. Key strengths include practical suggestions strongly tethered to Scripture and the recognition of real issues youth ministers are facing today and will face well into the future, such as the proliferation of technology and the lack of balance that results in failing to make rest a normal part of ministry. Drawing from a broad range of sources also strengthens the book making it appealing across denominational lines. Though no national consensus data exists in terms of youth pastor tenure, examples supporting the claim of an eighteen-month average would be helpful. That said, *Remodeling Youth Ministry* is well-researched, very well written, and is an excellent resource for youth pastors and others who desire to think about youth and family ministry differently. I highly recommend putting this book in the hands of all who serve in youth and family ministry.

A family-aligned curriculum
for every generation!

aligns all ages of the family

D6 CURRICULUM aligns small group environments at church so the entire family from kindergarten to grandparents, is studying the same theme at the same time. D62GEN helps parents and grandparents connect with kids and teens (even if they are miles away) through the use of devotional study guides, Splink, Home Connection, and other take-home resources that help equip the home.

D62Gen connects
the church and home through
generational discipleship.

www.d62gen.com

BASED ON DEUTERONOMY 6:5-9

THE JOURNAL OF
DISCIPLESHIP & FAMILY MINISTRY

The Journal of Discipleship and Family Ministry, a peer-reviewed journal based at The Southern Baptist Theological Seminary, is currently accepting abstract proposals for articles to be published in two forthcoming issues: (1) **Narrative and Christian Discipleship [Summer 2018]**, and (2) **Discipleship and Biblical Community [Fall/Winter 2018]**.

Submission Information

Proposal abstracts and completed articles should be submitted to Michael Graham, JDFM Managing Editor, via email [mgraham@sbts.edu].

Submission Deadlines

Narrative and Christian Discipleship

- Abstract proposal [500 words]: due May 15, 2018
- Completed article: due July 15, 2018

Discipleship and Biblical Community

- Abstract proposal [500 words]: due September 15, 2018
- Completed article: due November 15, 2018

Review Process:

The editorial staff will review all abstract proposals and invite selected authors to submit a completed article. Note: invitation to submit an article indicates the editors' *interest* in considering the article for publication, but does not confirm the article's *acceptance* for publication. All submitted articles undergo double-blind peer-review process as they are considered for acceptance, and as they are finalized for publication.

Editor

John David Trentham, Ph.D

Managing Editor

Michael Todd Graham Jr., Ph.D Candidate

Book Review Editor

Shane Parker, Ph.D

*For inquiries regarding formatting guidelines, please contact Michael Graham at mgraham@sbts.edu.

CPSIA information can be obtained
at www.ICGtesting.com
Printed in the USA
LVOW03s1254260418
574920LV00007B/14/P